Courageous Collaboration with Gracious Space

From Small Openings to Profound Transformation

By Patricia M. Hughes
Karma Ruder
Dale Nienow

Center for
Ethical Leadership

www.ethicalleadership.org

Courageous Collaboration with Gracious Space
From Small Openings to Profound Transformation

Graphic Design: Joshua Schramm
Cover Design: Leah Mitchell
Center for Ethical Leadership Executive Director: Dale Nienow

Published by the Center for Ethical Leadership
1401 East Jefferson St., Suite 505
Seattle, WA 98122
www.ethicalleadership.org

First Printing, June 2011

Printed in the United States of America
ISBN: 978-0-9755440-3-7

Book pages printed with soy bean ink on paper with
40% post-consumer recycled content.

About the Cover Design
Courageous Collaboration with Gracious Space invites us to play with possibility at a level that goes beyond the average cooperative effort or compromise. Courageous Collaboration issues a call and a challenge to bring our courage, intention and inspired hopes for a better world into being, now. The swirling design of finger paint represents the complexity and dynamic movement that often accompanies collaborative efforts, while the colors represent diverse viewpoints and the unique gifts of the players involved. Where they intertwine, new possibilities emerge. The white spaces within the pattern represent the small openings which, if nurtured, can yield profound transformation. The image assures us that Gracious Space can hold and guide our efforts as we move toward courageous collaboration and positive change.

Acknowledgments

The stirrings for this book began in the summer of 2007 when we realized we needed a collection of practical tools and activities to help guide practitioners in applying Gracious Space. We initially envisioned a field guide. From this beginning, we hosted several focus groups with friends and colleagues who helped us get a better bearing on the purpose of the book. Many thanks to those early supporters and listeners: Diane Altman-Dautoff, Malcolm Best, Shirley Blasé, Charlie Cunniff, Ron Gage, Sheri Herndon, Bernie Matsuno, Anne Nelson, Teresa Posakony, Michael Lindfield, and Bruce Takata. Their advice and imaginings for the potential of Gracious Space helped us see we needed much more than a tool kit.

Many thanks go to the Kellogg Foundation and the communities, coaches and partners engaged in the Kellogg Leadership for Community Change initiative. They brought Gracious Space deeply into their community practice and helped us learn how the elements of Gracious Space could form the foundation for a powerful and collaborative change model.

The development of the Gracious Space Change Framework took place over the course of three years, with many trainings, applications, retreats and conversations with practitioners across the country. Special acknowledgment goes to Humanities Montana, which made it possible to introduce Gracious Space to leaders and practitioners in Billings, Bozeman, Flathead Valley, Great Falls and Missoula, and to Horizon House, which embraced Gracious Space as a foundation for cultural change in its leadership and organizational life.

Readers of early book drafts include Diane Altman-Dautoff, Shasta Cano-Martin, Myrna Schlegel and Gayle D'Sousa Warner. Their enthusiasm and tactful questioning led us to ever deeper levels of clarity. We are also grateful to Bob Anderson, Francisco Guajardo and

Peggy Holman for taking time out of their busy lives to write about how Gracious Space has had a positive impact in their fields and communities, and to let us put that on the back cover!

Center staff member Melissa Hamasaki provided expert editing from inside the Center office, and Myrna Schlegel provided tremendously valuable editing, questioning and support from outside. Special thanks also go to Paul Schmidt who provided invaluable help with the development of certain ideas and writing, and to Leah Mitchell, who worked with us on several cover designs and creatively used the artwork of Mei Mei Peterson for inspiration. Staff member Steve Stapleton served in many capacities throughout the process, including as liaison through the publication process, and Joshua Schramm provided layout and production services.

A final word of gratitude goes to the hundreds of practitioners across the country, and increasingly around the world, who have sought new ways to lead and who have brought Gracious Space to life in some very contentious, diverse and challenging situations. We couldn't have written this book without your willingness to experiment and come along for the ride!

iii

Table of Contents

Introduction

Welcome to <u>Courageous Collaboration with Gracious Space: From Small Openings to Profound Transformation</u>. The Center is glad you are here, and we are excited to share what we have learned about using Gracious Space as a catalyst for human transformation and collaborative change.

For over ten years the Center for Ethical Leadership (CEL) has taught and shared the four core Gracious Space elements of spirit, setting, invite the 'stranger' and learn in public. The Center has engaged over 15,000 people in 30 states and 35 countries, helping to create Gracious Space in diverse settings such as schools, hospitals, churches, non-profit and community organizations, government agencies and businesses. Our first book, <u>Gracious Space: A practical guide for working better together</u>, has sold over 8,000 copies, is in its second edition and third printing, and has been used by hundreds of groups to forge deeper partnerships and collaborate better.

These people — whether acting as leaders, employees, citizens or family members — have found that Gracious Space enables them to have conversations that invite different backgrounds and ideas, emphasize respectful listening, and encourage an openness to working together. They have found that Gracious Space has the power to create a safe environment where different perspectives are welcome and where people can learn together rather than compete and defend.

When we reside at the level of politeness or civility, we avoid the truth telling that allows us to engage people and confront difficult organizational, community and societal issues at the deepest level. Friends in Minneapolis describe how Gracious Space helped them get past their culture of "Minnesota nice," which prevents them from talking about the real issues. Colleagues from the South say Gracious Space enabled them to get beyond the "southern hospitality" which can get in the way of expressing real views. They have found that Gracious Space can support their most adversarial conversations.

As we have deepened the use of Gracious Space in diverse settings, we have found that the four elements of Gracious Space can be directly applied to dynamic change processes. This book describes the Gracious Space Change Framework, a collaborative model we have developed that enables change agents and groups to apply the transformative insights and processes of Gracious Space to change efforts.

We have identified four key components that affect every change process: the energetic state of the group, the concrete actions of the group, the inner life of the change agent and the inner life of the group as an entity. The four elements of Gracious Space – spirit, setting, invite the 'stranger' and learn in public – help us view those components of change in a way that makes it easier to figure out what is working and what is not in the change process. In the Framework, the four elements become a lens and a diagnostic tool through which to view change. The four elements also form a container to hold the dynamics of any change process. Finally, the four elements form a set of strategies that can remedy problems, address issues, and give shape to creative and practical thinking. This book explores the resulting dynamics and possibilities.

The Gracious Space Change Framework is a robust methodology. In a Gracious Space-infused change process, people develop deep and trusting relationships, work across boundaries and differences, share diverse perspectives, develop shared purpose, work through conflict, discover transformative solutions, carry out emerging ideas for change, and adapt as needed throughout the process. Use of the Gracious Space Change Framework can open people to unprecedented transformation, channel efforts into shared purpose and action, and help groups, organizations and societies reach solutions at their highest potential. This book provides a much-needed pathway to inspire and activate collaborative change.

The Need for an Integral and Collaborative Approach to Change

Throughout history people have tended to undertake change

work either by using the analytical and logical tools of the mind, or by pursuing a more relational approach we associate with the heart. This is also true in the world of management and leadership: there are supporters of more scientific models and advocates of more relational models.

While both approaches contain wisdom, neither is completely adequate to explain how things actually happen in human systems like organizations, communities or families. The need for new models of change that enable both the heart space of deep partnerships and the mind space of strategic, tangible steps, is critical and growing. When we say the Gracious Space Change Framework is integral in its approach to change, we are referring to its ability to engage both heart and mind at deep levels.

Surely we stand at a time in history when leaders must lead in a more integrated and collaborative way. Our institutions and systems are increasingly ineffective at serving the majority of people. In today's dominant culture we are very focused on moving to action, making an impact, solving problems and fixing things. Given the times we are living in, we need better ways of living and we need them now.

We need to mend and re-orient our approaches. We need to solve problems permanently rather than offering temporary band-aids. Yet, if we move too quickly to answers, we lose the possibility of getting outside our own boxes and run the risk of simply repeating what hasn't worked before in bigger ways.

Rather than rushing off to do something, perhaps we should reflect for a moment on what matters most. What will help us make the shifts we collectively need to make? What has the potential to open up radically new possibilities? What actions will make the most difference? The Gracious Space Change Framework can help answer these questions and make the necessary shifts, because Gracious Space creates room for the collective wisdom essential for discovering a better way. This book guides leaders and change agents through an innovative and collaborative change model, and is an invitation to step into transformational change more intentionally and effectively, to better serve our collective good.

Many experts and practitioners over the past few years have advocated for integrated and collaborative leadership approaches. Peter Block, one of the gurus of leadership and management, wrote in

Community: The Structure of Belonging, "If we maintain the old conversations about making the world predictable, measurable, individual-focused, and leader-driven, nothing will change. Our work is to overcome the culture of isolation, fear, and waiting for the leaders to get their act together. This occurs when we shift the conversation from problem solving to possibility, deficiencies and needs to gifts, and blame and barter to ownership and commitment."

Dr. Rosabeth Moss Kanter, professor at Harvard Business School, told a conference of community leaders that it's time for a new leadership lexicon built on noble purpose, shared values and partnerships. The noble purpose is the reason for our work; values form the glue that holds us together; and partnerships, especially between non-profits and for-profits, make real and sustainable change happen. "The new leadership lexicon is all about finding permanent solutions to the big problems rather than just helping people deal with the problems better," Dr. Kanter said.

His Holiness the Dalai Lama has said that compassion is key to childhood development and lasting peace. Visiting Seattle for The Seeds of Compassion conference, the Dalai Lama presided over five days of dialogues intended to nurture kindness and compassion in the world, starting with children and all who touch their lives. The gathering highlighted compelling research about the role compassion plays in the development of children. The Dalai Lama noted with some humor that compassion would benefit grown-ups, too. He has also said that the next Buddha would come not as an individual, but as a compassionate community.

The W.K. Kellogg Foundation, a longtime leader in the field of individual leadership development, recently established a shared leadership program, believing that this approach will create more permanent and sustainable change than individual leadership. They concluded the wildly popular Kellogg Leadership Fellows program and started the Kellogg Leadership for Community Change (KLCC) program which explored the possibilites of collective leadership. The KLCC program provided three years of initial support to eleven communities across the country working for positive change in education and youth-adult partnerships. The Center for Ethical Leadership served as intermediary in developing and implementing the program, and continues to support the community work through the national Community Learning Exchange.

Finally, C. Otto Scharmer writes in <u>Theory U: Leading from the Future as it Emerges</u>, "We live in a time of massive institutional failure, collectively creating results that nobody wants... destruction of communities, nature, life – the foundations of our social, economic, ecological, and spiritual well-being. This time calls for a new consciousness and a new collective leadership capacity to meet challenges in a more conscious, intentional, and strategic way. The development of such a capacity would allow us to create a future of greater possibilities."

So here we are. We find ourselves in phenomenally diverse communities facing confounding choices. We have an immense need for developing shared values, strong partnerships, courageous collaboration, continuous learning and overt compassion. We have a great need to imagine and implement positive change. And to enable all that to happen, we need a way to hold our differences, dialogues and dreams so that we dare to articulate and create positive futures together to dramatically improve our lives. Gracious Space can serve as that container. Gracious Space can help us understand the components of change and create strategies that work. The Gracious Space Change Framework introduced in this book builds on the transformative elements of Gracious Space to provide a powerful and proven methodology for engaging the heart and mind in deep and lasting change.

Ultimately our need for a better way of being together brings us to questions of human development. How are we evolving as a species? What is our next big learning as human beings? We believe the ability to work more collaboratively and live more compassionately with each other is unfolding as a frontier of human development. We believe humans are evolving toward increasing willingness and ability to get along without killing, hurting, blaming or shaming. Although there are plenty of instances where violent interactions still occur, our species is, in general, improving our capacity to behave in more effective and agreeable ways. We are learning to work better together to achieve common goals that nurture and sustain life.

Collaborative and compassionate leadership is the work of our time. There is an old saying, "If you can dream it, you can do it." Of course, much hard work lies between dreaming and doing. After we dream "it," we need to put "it" into noble and compelling terms, then create environments for strengthening the emotional life of the group, align partners around shared passion and purpose, engage in reflection and in learning about individual and group patterns, be collaborative and creative, then we can do "it." While we engage in doing "it," we need tools to gather diverse ideas, brainstorm positive solutions and move ahead together. We need to learn how to navigate uncertainty, take risks and move in unknown, but potentially enormously creative, territory. The new leadership is about integrating mind and heart, and collaboratively bringing innovative solutions to the challenging issues of the day.

Peter Drucker, the original management guru, said that leadership powers human progress; it is "the organ that converts a mob into an organization and human effort into performance." To the thousands of people working in their own ways to advance the collective good, we humbly and hopefully offer <u>Courageous Collaboration with Gracious Space: From Small Openings to Profound Transformation</u>.

Run Toward the Roar

We want to let readers know right away that implementing the Gracious Space Change Framework is rewarding yet rigorous work. It is not a change model for the faint of heart or uncommitted. In fact, an alternate title for this book could be <u>Gracious Space: Are You Strong Enough?</u> Using the Gracious Space Change Framework requires us to be deeply committed to developing our own capacity and that of our groups, to move into unknown territory, and create a collective approach to change in uncertainty and ambiguity.

A popular folk tale from Africa reveals the truth about working in fearful times and venturing into risky territory.

On the African savannahs the lion is the most feared hunter. When lions hunt, an old, weak member of the pride moves away from the hunting pack. Having lost most of his teeth, the old male's roar is greater than his ability to bite. The old one settles in the grass and waits.

When the herds enter the area between the hunting pack and the old lion, the old male roars mightily. When antelopes hear the sound of a lion's roar, their instinct tells them to run in the opposite direction, away from the source of fear. But this is just what the lions expect them to do...and they have anticipated that the

*antelopes will run straight toward the lionesses lying in
ambush across from the roaring male.
When the lion roars, the herd runs right into the jaws of
the waiting hunters.*

*So the old people of the villages used to tell the
children, "If you are on the savannah and hear the roar,
run toward the roar," for there you will find safety and
a way through.*

In every organization, community or group of people, there are
times when our happiness or security feel threatened, and our natural
reaction is to run the other way. But sooner or later we find the threats
returning and compounding. Effective leaders realize that survival,
success and safety come from going toward the place where the fear
seems to originate, and having the courage to confront threats. In his
book, The World Behind the World, Michael Meade reflects on this folk
tale and what it means for people seeking a meaningful path through
life. "Those who seek security in a rapidly changing world run right
into the teeth of one dilemma or another," Meade writes. "It might be
better to run toward the roar and learn what it means to live in a time
of many endings."

Using the Gracious Space Change Framework to its greatest potential is about developing individual and group capacity to run toward
the roar, to inquire into the unknown, to advance creative and positive
change, even in the face of unpredictability and fear. Leaders of organizations and community efforts are committed not just to survival, but
to innovation and sustainability. So how do we thrive in a world that
is unraveling? How do we have the hard conversations without being
hard on each other? How do we manage while our systems are falling
apart?

The Gracious Space Change Framework presented in this book
can help. It can hold the most pressing and dynamic change processes
and the full complexity of communities and organizations. The Change
Framework opens people up and makes transformation more likely.
Remember: it only takes a small opening for profound change to occur.

Before setting out, we need to remind readers that Gracious
Space — whether applied as attention to the four elements or within
the more complex context of the Change Framework — cannot easily transform certain kinds of organizations, communities or groups.

Groups intent on maintaining a status quo steeped in hierarchy, power dynamics and rigid belief systems may not be ready for the type of collaborative change Gracious Space invites, and will require patience and small beginnings. Gracious Space is most potent when the organization espouses and embodies the values of mutual respect, compassion, reflective learning and collaborative action. That said, we also know that hard environments are often the ones that most need Gracious Space.

Gracious Space can breathe life into any setting. While we are engaged in essential and demanding work, it is important to take care of ourselves. Gracious Space is nurturing; it encourages learning and innovating. Gracious Space can help us lighten up and explore creativity in joyful and lively ways with others. When we feel playful, we are more open to surprising ideas. This refreshing space opens our minds and hearts so we can more easily grasp the fresh and unexpected insights that result.

How to Use This Book

We wrote this book to provide inspiration and practical support to leaders, change agents, consultants, facilitators and others navigating change processes. We wrote this book for people actively participating in our human evolution toward collaborative, sustainable and positive change, offering this methodology so we might all get there faster with fewer setbacks. The book combines theory with practice: there is an overview of the Gracious Space Change Framework, as well as tools, activities, examples and case studies that will enable groups to leverage the Framework to its highest use.

Our intentions here are to:

- Deepen understanding and use of the core elements of Gracious Space;
- Present the Gracious Space Change Framework and the key components of change;
- Demonstrate how the Change Framework enables collaborative change;
- Provide tools and activities to accelerate the use of Gracious Space in change processes around the world;
- Invite readers to join the national Gracious Space Practitioners network.

Part One: The Gracious Space Change Framework

Chapter One: Deepening the Foundation of the Four Elements. This chapter revisits the four core elements (Spirit, Setting, Invite the 'Stranger' and Learn in Public) introduced in the first book on Gracious Space. We invite readers to learn about and/or deepen their understanding of these elements, by including a definition, describing dimensions to show the multiple facets of the each element, and providing examples and stories of how we have put them into practice in various settings.

Chapter Two: Stepping into the Field of Change. There are many theories about how change happens, and it is not the intention of this book to review or evaluate all of those. Rather, in this chapter we explore change as a process that bridges what is known and what is unknown. We explore the aspects of known and unknown territory, invite readers to explore their relationship to the known and unknown aspects of change, and help readers assess their own change work.

Chapter Three: Overview of the Gracious Space Change Framework. This chapter provides an overview of the Framework, introducing the four key components that affect every change process: the energetic state of the group, the concrete actions of the group, the inner life of the change agent and the inner life of the group as an entity.

Chapter Four: The Four Openings. This chapter, and the three that follow, delve more deeply into the Gracious Space Change Framework. Chapter Four describes the Four Openings in the Framework: Opening to Safety, Opening to Relationship, Opening to Risk and Opening to Collective Creativity. These are the energetic states of a group as it advances in its ability to create Gracious Space and run toward the roar together. Through narrative and examples, we explain the Four Openings, why they matter, what blocks the openings and when and how to move forward.

Chapter Five: The Four Stages of Change. A good change framework contains concrete, strategic actions leaders must take to enact change. These actions serve both as benchmarks and goals. This chapter defines the four primary stages of change within the Gracious Space Change Framework: Build Trust, Co-Construct Purpose and Plans, Act Together, and Sustain the Work. Through narrative and examples, we describe the Four Stages of Change, why they matter, and how to move through them.

Chapter Six: Practice of the Change Agent. The quality of any change is related to the inner work of the change agent. Chapter Six demonstrates how the change agent, in order to best serve the group, must pay attention to his or her own patterns, readiness, and level of comfort with the unknown and with change processes. This chapter suggests ways the change agent can be more mindful about how he or she shows up, why that matters, and how to translate that awareness into greater likelihood of success for the group.

Chapter Seven: Work of the Group. Many groups trying to advance change simply stick to the strategic tasks at hand. The Gracious Space Change Framework illuminates the inner life of the group that must be attended to in order to reach truly collaborative and sustained innovation. This chapter outlines the skill sets of building a relational field, identifying common group patterns, reinforcing positive patterns, and shifting patterns that cause groups to be stuck.

Part Two: The Field Guide

Chapter Eight: Assessing and Developing Readiness. This chapter helps the change agent assess a group's readiness to engage with Gracious Space as a change process. This includes assessing the group's strengths, considering whether the group culture is open, neutral or hard, and identifying and developing pockets of openness within the culture that can be leveraged to give Gracious Space a chance.

Chapter Nine: Case Studies. This chapter presents seven case studies that detail very diverse change engagements that used Gracious Space. The cases demonstrate the initial assessment, the design of what we did and why, and what happened as a result. This chapter also describes seven shorter examples of how Gracious Space was more simply applied to enact positive change. Finally, the chapter gives an overview of Evidence-Based Practice survey data on the impact of Gracious Space in communities and organizations.

Chapter Ten: Tools and Activities to Establish Gracious Space. This chapter contains 30 ways to establish Gracious Space, ranging from simple to more complex activities. We examine the role of inquiry in activating successful change, and also invite readers to become Gracious Space Practitioners in connection with the Center for Ethical Leadership. Visit www.ethicalleadership.org now to learn more about these tools and the Center and Gracious Space.

Let's Begin!

So again, welcome. You are now part of the on-going and co-evolving story of Gracious Space. You can help spread and deepen the use of Gracious Space and "put the legs on" an integrated approach to leadership and the advancement of collaborative, positive change. We hope you will take what you learn from these pages and join us in helping to move organizations and communities forward, together, with deeper understanding and generative, positive solutions. Your practical applications of the material in this book will help advance the body of work now shared and practiced by thousands of leaders and organizations worldwide.

Part One

The Gracious Space Change Framework

"All positive change in the world comes from our ideas of what we believe is possible."
— *Alexandra Jamieson*

Part One of this book lays the theoretical foundation of collaborative change within Gracious Space. The Gracious Space Change Framework offers a useful, visionary and robust model for change that blends heart, mind and spirit and supports individuals, organizations and communities in their work for positive change in the world.

The Gracious Space Change Framework provides a means to open the self and group to what is possible in service of personal evolution and the greater good. The work of our times is to co-create the future. Courageous Collaboration with Gracious Space invites participants to question what's not working, open the door to collective leadership and enter into a process of deep caring. This process enables practitioners of Gracious Space to be receptive to great potential and puts them in a position to catalyze unprecedented change in themselves and the world.

By courageous collaboration we mean being willing to be "all in" — to show up with all of our gifts and all of our questions. Too often collaboration is an approach of "you do yours and I'll do mine and we'll try not to get in each other's way." Today's collaborative efforts often are negotiations rather than new creations born out of what has most heart and most meaning. To practice courageous collaboration is to commit ourselves to something that is worthy of our whole selves. And, we invite others to show up in the same way. From that new place different possibilities emerge.

The Gracious Space Change Framework creates room for courageous collaboration, along with practical ideas for how to help move together through dynamic change. Part One contains seven chapters and eight worksheets to help change agents thoroughly understand this process. We hope this section inspires and motivates readers to unleash their full imaginative potential as we all work to make the positive changes our communities and organizations long for.

Chapter One

Deepening the Foundation of the Four Elements

"If you have a strong foundation, then you can build or rebuild anything on it. But if you've got a weak foundation you can't build anything."

—Jack Scalia

The Center's first book on Gracious Space provided an introduction to the four elements of Gracious Space: a *spirit and setting where we invite the 'stranger' and learn in public.* In this chapter we offer a more complex explanation of each element and provide examples of how we have activated them in various settings with our partners and allies. The purposes of doing this are to introduce the core elements to anyone who has not read the first book, to establish a shared vocabulary, and begin to identify the potential of the core elements to engage with change. To begin with, we've affirmed that:

- People are hungry for Gracious Space, and sometimes just saying the words can have a transforming effect;

- The four core elements of Gracious Space introduced in 2004 — spirit, setting, invite the 'stranger' and learn in public — continue to resonate;

- The essential concepts of Gracious Space are as old as humankind, yet without a framework, people tend not to act on them;

- Groups who are most successful using Gracious Space adapt the terminology to fit their unique culture;

- Gracious Space is a catalyst for unprecedented collaboration, helping people cross boundaries and engage in breakthrough thinking previously inaccessible or unimaginable; and

- Gracious Space can be taught in five minutes, yet it can take a lifetime to master.

The Center for Ethical Leadership has worked in many difficult situations where Gracious Space has proven to be effective. As groups are willing to go deeper and have the challenging conversations that previously prevented them from moving forward, Gracious Space has provided a safe and supportive container for building trust and relationships, and opportunities for newly imagined possibilities.

Through the process of creating Gracious Space, people are asked to bring their best spirit and intentions and to establish ways of working together that allow the group to do its most significant work. Gracious Space can be established quickly, but the true test of its strength comes when it is called on to help the group stick together during difficult conversations about difference and misunderstanding. It is in this way that Gracious Space invites the group and each member to open up to transformation.

For example, in Buffalo, New York a community group that was part of the national Kellogg Leadership for Community Change (KLCC) initiative committed to improving teaching and learning in their schools. At the time, the school district was facing bankruptcy. The community had been denied federal funding for after-school programs because of the inability of various agencies to work together. Buffalo also had a history of being divided by race and ethnicities in various neighborhoods. It was in this environment that the KLCC Fellows intentionally formed a group of 25 people who represented the diversity of the city and started to seek collaboration.

A short time later, they attended a national conference with other KLCC communities. Each group was asked to introduce their community and work. Buffalo chose to do this through a video. As the Buffalo fellow presented the video to the group in preparation for the gathering, instead of receiving affirmation for taking on this project, she received criticism. "That is not the way I see my community," participants said. "Why did you show only the boarded up houses in my neighborhood?"

In that moment the Buffalo group realized they had very different perspectives about the strengths and challenges of their own neighborhoods and didn't understand each other's experiences. They realized that some of these differences in perspectives were related to issues of race and class. When they encountered this profound tension, they could have split apart, but instead, they chose to practice Gracious Space and keep building relationships that could handle meaningful change work. Gracious Space provided a container that was strong enough to handle the difficult dynamics of conversations about race and class and how their different experiences would impact their change process. "The KLCC Fellows used Gracious Space to deal with major trust issues and work better together," said Ceylane Myers, coach for the Buffalo Fellows.

The group ultimately facilitated negotiations among a number of agencies, the school district, and the city to reach agreement for how to use federal funds to support a vibrant spectrum of after-school programs, resulting in $1.5 million in new funding.

The Four Elements

Spirit

When we speak of spirit, we mean intentionally building a supportive atmosphere or holding environment for the work. Many of us have experienced being in groups where the tone of the gathering starts negatively and spirals down from there. In the book Social Intelligence, Daniel Goleman suggests that "a mood can spread through a group with great rapidity." How we show up is contagious; the mood "infects" others and spreads throughout the group. If the energy is negative, negativity will spread. If the energy is positive, creativity and optimism will spread. The element of spirit has three dimensions.

❖   **Dimension 1: The spirit we bring. We can "be" Gracious Space based on the spirit we carry into each interaction.** Being the spirit of Gracious Space means bringing our best stuff to every interaction. Will we bring openness and a willingness to collaborate? Or will we come to the meeting filled with prejudgments and close-minded certainty about others or the project?

Sometimes when we anticipate meeting with someone who is difficult to work with, a tape starts playing in our heads. "Why do I have to have another meeting with this person? I'll just try to get through it." These kinds of thoughts will likely lead to a self fulfilling prophecy of an unproductive and painful experience. With a little preparation, we can change the tape. When working with someone who is challenging for us, we can remind ourselves to assume goodwill — that they mean well — and to look for their gifts. This helps us listen to what they are saying with less judgment and more understanding.

Bringing a spirit of Gracious Space requires warming up, the same as an athlete would for a big game or a musician would for a performance. Athletes stretch and musicians play the scales; they don't just charge out and expect to do their best work. The truth is we all could benefit from some warming up. Most of us can't just roll out of bed and be brilliant, especially if any kind of learning, diverse opinion or conflict is involved. So what practices can we use to ready ourselves for each day and the challenges we will face? How do we become centered in our best gifts and intentions? How do we show up with a helpful spirit to be fully present to others?

Taking the time to get centered and choosing a few attributes of Gracious Space to embody can be the difference between joy and frustration. Starting a meeting with three breaths is a simple way for the leader and the group to prepare for the day's work. It's no accident that the root of the word breath, *inspirare*, can also be found in the words inspiration and spirit. To breathe means to inspire with spirit. We can also refresh our awareness of spirit by taking the Gracious Space Self-Assessment (found at the end of this chapter) and claiming our best gifts.

Freedom is the pause between stimulus and action. In the moment after something occurs and before we react, we are free to choose how we will show up. What will you choose?

❖   **Dimension 2: The spirit we create together in a group.** Whenever people come together they create a field of energy that is the combination of their individual spirits and intentions. This field can be shaped purposefully or left to form on its own. Too often groups make the mistake of assuming that getting down to business is the most effective way of using their time together. They fail to intentionally create a positive learning environment. They fail to acknowledge all the many distractions people carry in their heads — family issues, work deadlines, car troubles, etc. — that prevent them from being fully attentive to the work of the group. They ignore opportunities to cultivate relationships that will better support the work.

The spirit of Gracious Space reminds us to be deliberate about creating supportive fields in our meetings and gatherings. This can be as simple as taking a moment of silence and asking people to let go of the distractions in their heads. Sometimes we ask, "What energy are you bringing into this group?" When people bring challenging energy, this question gives them the chance to release it. When they bring positive energy this can spread to others. This may take only a few minutes at the beginning, and can smooth the way for more authentic interactions. Every group that is together for a while develops a personality. What makes this group different from the one down the street? Paying attention to the spirit of the group will help ensure this personality is beneficial, not detrimental, to the people and the work.

❖   **Dimension 3: A greater spirit we can tap into.** There is a larger consciousness or energy beyond that of any group or gathering which provides a context and can be a resource for the work. Sometimes the greater spirit is the mission of the organization or project. Sometimes the greater spirit is something that defines our times. For example, the civil rights and women's rights movements of the 1960s and 70s created a consciousness of freeing society from limits and inequalities. This consciousness swept the nation. Today, sustainability and an awareness of our interdependence — as we see how connected we are in the world — informs our larger consciousness. We do not have to be religious to believe there is a larger, underlying energy and spirit for good that contributes to our human experience.

This larger spirit can also be closely tied to physical place through events and history that have occurred there. People visiting the Ground Zero site of the Twin Towers in New York experience an overwhelming sense of the greater spirit of that place. This can happen at Gettysburg, the Lincoln monument, or wherever there is a tangible feeling of a major shift that transformed the relationships of the people there. It is a very powerful act to tap into this larger spirit and consciously connect it to the purpose of the group. This imprints a particular aspect of spirit on the gathering.

For example, the Center convened a diverse group of 180 community members from across the United States at Stone Mountain, near Atlanta, Georgia, for three days of dialogue on how to build more just communities. Stone Mountain is the site of the rebirth of the Ku Klux Klan in the early 1900s, and is near the home of the Martin Luther King Jr. Center and the Carter Center, so this was a place with a palpable relationship to the greater spirit of justice.

To tap into that greater spirit, we asked the planning group to meditate on the spirit of justice for thirty days prior to the event. Upon arrival, we asked one member of the group to tour the city and immerse herself in the unique spirit of justice in Atlanta. She visited the Martin Luther King Jr. Center to learn more about his work in civil rights. She visited The Carter Center to see President Carter's global work for justice and toured the Stone Mountain visitor center. The afternoon before all the participants arrived, she shared what she had learned about justice from each site. Her impressions and stories connected the planning team to the larger spirit of overcoming injustice that was embedded in this place. The rest of the planning team added their hopes about justice for our conference. This clear focus on justice imprinted a powerful spirit leading to a highly successful conference.

Setting

Setting includes the time allotted for the meeting as well as the physical space where it takes place. Attending to this element requires paying attention to the type of interaction we want to support.

❖ **Dimension 1: The approach needs to fit the goal of the interaction.** The approach has to do both with time (how much you have) and design (how information is imparted). It is important to know the purpose of the gathering and to plan a physical space, agenda and approach that support that purpose. Here's a story from a colleague that demonstrates the importance of the approach.

> *"When my wife and I were first married, we commuted together. The first year of marriage was filled with conversations about how we would live out the relationship. There were lots of adjustments. We would chat on our way into work and my wife would drop me off at my office and then drive to her work place. Sometimes just as I was stepping out of the car, she would say, "I've been thinking..." This signaled that a Conversation with a capital "C" was about to take place.*
>
> *Suspended in step, I didn't know what to do. I was anxious to get to my new job and I also wanted to attend to the relationship with my new wife. When we got home, we talked and decided we needed to make sure we had conversations in the right place with enough time for that particular issue. We created the shorthand saying 'No curbside conversations.'"*

Inappropriate approaches happen often. For example, many times by the end of a meeting, a group finally arrives at the discussion that matters most, but they are out of time to adequately address it. We need to anticipate the time needed to warm up a group to be ready for the important discussions, and then to provide a sufficient space for the conversation to occur.

❖   **Dimension 2: Attend to the physical space.** Choosing the space for a meeting or gathering is an important decision because physical space influences the way we feel. What makes a space supportive for good human interaction? Natural lighting, room to move, comfortable chairs, ability to see others, good acoustics, food, convenient restrooms... This list can go on. If we want to foster an engaging interaction among participants, requiring them to sit in fixed chairs in a lecture hall is a mismatch.

Many times we have been in a space ill-suited to the purpose of the meeting. One of the worst examples was a day-long outplacement seminar for hospital staff who had just learned their jobs were eliminated. The meeting was held in a cramped, windowless basement room, just past the furnace and directly next to a room labeled "The Morgue." For people who might have benefitted from a bit of compassion, this was not the right space for this meeting! Too often we stifle the potential of our interactions by convening in sterile, unimaginative, rigid, and unwelcoming spaces. It helps to find space that is flexible and allows facilitators to adjust the set-up for different parts of the gathering.

We once worked with a business group that had low levels of trust and wanted to make some changes. We met in a hotel meeting space, typically not an ideal "gracious" space, but it was off-site in order to break them from their normal routines. The room had natural lighting and was big enough to allow for some different seating configurations.

We started with no tables in the room, only chairs. This was intended to keep the tables from being a barrier and to create an openness that could lead to different possibilities. We met in a semi-circle where we could easily break into pairs for story telling. There was enough space to set up side tables for work groups to sketch out ideas. We used the walls around the semi-circle to post their ideas about trust and the work could be easily seen by everyone. There was plenty of room to move, thus reinforcing the concept of getting unstuck and moving forward. Participants all wrote something on the summary chart, which helped them each connect to creating a different direction going forward. The creative use of this meeting space supported the creation of new patterns of interaction. At the end of the meeting, they said, "We let down our guard and opened up to possibilities."

It is effective to ask participants the question, "What changes that we can control will make this space more gracious?" The group can then reshape the room to suit their needs. At the Center office, we previously had one long table in the conference room bolted to the floor. It offered no flexibility so we removed this table and replaced it with three square tables. They can be configured into one large board table, a medium sized conference table or three smaller tables. We scale the size of the table to the number of participants in the meeting so everyone feels more intimately connected. We can also move all the tables quickly to the end of the room and form a circle of chairs to support a dialogue. In the course of a two- or three-hour meeting, we often vary the configuration of the room. Our board members now know they can request a change at any point they want to shift the interaction.

❖   **Dimension 3: Add physical objects to enhance the space.**
We cannot always control the room we will be in, but there are always ways to change the feel of the space by bringing additional objects. Sometimes little touches can make a big difference. Add a tablecloth or colorful scarf to the registration table. Bring flowers to welcome participants. Create a harvest basket of fall vegetables. Set objects on the tables that invite exploration and connection — sea glass, feathers, shells, and rocks. Sea glass is a symbol of transformation. Glass is made partly from sand, then the glass is returned to the sea which smoothes out the sharp edges, and finally it returns to the beach as a gift of beauty for people to hold in their hands. Explain the meaning of the items or simply provide them as a source of curiosity, creativity or grounding. Holding a stone as we think deeply about an issue can provide grounding and connection.

Many of us have had meetings in rooms the shape and character of a box. In these situations, we often involve the participants in creating the environment by posting work on the walls and shaping the character of the space during the course of the day. For instance, we have started meetings by taking pictures of participants with a Polaroid camera and posting them along with some description of where they grew up and a few items of interest such as what they do for fun and their favorite book. Decorating the wall with forty pictures immediately brings diversity and personal interest into the room.

In our conference room we posted the definition of Gracious Space on the wall. Regardless of the focus of the meeting, people can notice the definition during the meeting and remind themselves to bring these elements into the work. We also have a tabletop fountain that provides a peaceful background to meetings. In the fountain are several descending steps made of small, flat stones. Written on the stones are the values people have said they are bringing to various gatherings we have hosted. This waterfall always brings out the curiosity and peacefulness of guests.

Invite the 'Stranger'

Invite the 'stranger' means to seek out the "other." In today's world, we are highly interdependent and need to stay connected to each other. When the path is uncertain or not one we have traveled before, we need input from multiple perspectives. Narrow group membership can lead to "group think" or unchallenged thinking which is dangerous to the vitality of any enterprise. With the rich diversity of our world we need to be more intentional in working with differences of all kinds including ideology, age, geography, race, class, education, religion, gender, and sexual orientation.

❖   **Dimension 1: Who needs to be in the room?** When groups come together to work on a shared purpose, it is important to determine the other perspectives needed to truly address the work at hand. It is not uncommon for leaders in positions of power to make decisions without input from stakeholders. Senior leaders in organizations frequently make decisions about solutions even though employees know much more about the actual content of what is needed.

Making assumptions and decisions without diverse input limits our thinking and possibilities for creative action. It also increases the risk of not getting buy-in or incorrectly assessing others' needs. Rather, we need to welcome different points of view as suggested by Peter Senge when he said: "When you hear a point of view that you disagree with, that is a window of opportunity to understand the system better."

A university president was interested in addressing the needs of commuter students who seemed to have less support and connection to the institution than students living on campus. Usually, he would have consulted the top dozen leaders in the college to identify potential solutions. Instead, he invited staff from all levels of the university to join in a discussion about commuter students.

The first ideas were directed at the types of intellectual discussions they could host for commuter students. Then an administrative assistant in one of the offices spoke up. "Students who live on campus can return to their rooms between classes. When commuter students come to my building, they hang out near my desk because there is a couch. They like to relax or sleep between classes." Her insight led to the creation of multiple small living rooms around campus each with its own unique identity shaped by the groups of commuter students who joined to form small communities in each place. An invitation to commuter students to join the discussion would have expanded the voice of the 'stranger' even further.

Even when we invite the other, it may sometimes take them time to respond. Have you noticed that when you ask children a question or invite their participation they may shy away? If you push, they will recede. But if you stay near and at their level, they will eventually come to you. Adults are the same way — we often need a little time to adjust to the invitation. But too frequently we give adults only one shot. We think, "Well, I made the invitation and he didn't take it. I tried. It's his choice and I'm done." Instead we need to give them time to respond in their own way. Gracious Space encourages us to make multiple invitations over time.

❖   **Dimension 2: See the 'stranger' as an opportunity to learn.** When we bring diversity into any group, the differences will eventually show up as tension and conflict. To be serious about creating Gracious Space, we need to be able to work with others we find difficult. Why bother with this? *Because we can't know everything.* We can't see all perspectives and possibilities from our single viewing point. It is important to be open to different approaches, ideologies, and world views. This does not mean we should accept harmful behavior or stay in a relationship that is abusive, but it does mean that we need to be more open-minded.

We have found it useful to reframe how we think of challenging situations or people. Asking, "What can I learn from this individual," or, "What does this situation have to teach me at this time?" can change the way we approach these situations. It is one thing to invite the 'stranger' and make room for their contributions. It is another thing entirely to open ourselves to being impacted by these contributions, to really let the 'stranger' get inside and transform us.

❖   **Dimension 3: Welcome the 'stranger' inside us.** When we take the time to reflect on our lives, we often discover struggles that take place inside us. We may identify a part of ourselves that we do not like so much, or an approach or pattern we repeatedly fall into that is not effective. Gracious Space invites us to engage in self reflection and identify the 'stranger' within us, and to make peace with those parts of ourselves.

It can help to ask, "What do I carry inside that is an old story, that is not really me or that I am ready to let go? What aspects of myself do I avoid? What behaviors get in the way of my best gifts and how I really want to live?" Paying attention to the 'stranger' within is a crucial aspect of creating Gracious Space for ourselves and others.

Learn in Public

Learning in public means letting go and opening up to possibilities. If we are to create new possibilities from our interactions with others, we need to be willing to make shifts that create openings. When we hold tightly to our viewpoints we crowd out any ability to be influenced by others. When we hold closely to our own expertise, we stop listening to the helpful insights in others' experiences. We need to unlearn the patterns of interaction that are unproductive. This frees us to discover more creative options together with others. Gracious Space encourages us to go through the process of unlearning, discovering, and relearning.

❖   **Dimension 1: Suspend judgment and explore assumptions.** Our judgments and assumptions about others lock them (and us) into a rigid box. They lead us to create stereotypes of others that cannot adequately portray the other person. Acting on rigid images of others ensures that we will get the results we expect because we haven't created any openings for the interaction to be different. When we suspend our judgments temporarily it creates room to explore assumptions and to understand others better. Imagine casting a fishing line into the water. You hook something and pull it up. You look at it. This is what we mean by suspending judgment — literally hang it out there to examine. Is the assumption or judgment you are having a helpful one? Is it worth keeping? Or should you throw it back? Being able to suspend judgment and explore assumptions enables us to listen differently and to actually learn something new.

When Seattle Public Schools hired John Stanford, a new superintendent with a military background and no education experience, it would have been easy for the teachers union to make assumptions about what to expect. It was the shared task of the head of the teachers union, Roger Erskine, and the superintendent to shape the collective bargaining agreement with teachers, often a contentious situation.

At the first meeting, John and Roger sized each other up. Roger recalls feeling the typical power dynamics expressed in the way the superintendent positioned himself formally behind the desk. Then Roger said, "I don't want to approach negotiations in the typical way. I want to try a different approach where we talk about what is most important about educating children and find common ground." John breathed a sigh of relief and said, "I want to do it differently also."

For a year they entered into a joint venture to significantly rewrite the teacher's contract. The discussions were framed around their shared values, and no contract language was written until the discussions were complete. "We shared a deep commitment to the importance of value-based relationships to the children, parents and staff of the Seattle Public Schools," Roger said. "It was, and still is, a very wonderful part of my career."

These two leaders created a small space that opened up tremendous possibilities. As we have learned, it only takes a small space to create the opening for profound transformation. We call these *spaces of grace.*

❖   **Dimension 2: Take risks.** It can be hard to admit we need help or don't know the right answer, particularly if we have a position of responsibility. In many work environments, the culture doesn't support making mistakes or taking risks. People who try new things and succeed may be rewarded; but people who try new things and fail are written up. So people are afraid to try new things, or they are afraid they will be discovered to be less capable than they need to be. Because these are such common fears, when one person takes risks it can open the space for others to do the same.

One manager in a large public utility told us a story of making a decision for her team that didn't work out. When she learned of Gracious Space, she went back to her team and said, "My decision didn't work very well. We all need to work together to come up with a better solution." And they did. What is more, her willingness to take a risk led her team to be more willing and able to take risks with each other.

❖   **Dimension 3: Deal with our own learning.** As people come together to solve problems or work on difficult issues, they often have a tendency to see the problem as "them," and if only "they" would change behaviors or positions, we could find the solution. We adopt an approach of "fixing others." The reality is we all play a part in these interactions, and we can't fix others, but we can change ourselves.

In group settings, we have found two powerful reflection questions help us identify our own learning edges, that is, those qualities or attitudes that keep us stuck. The first is, "What do I need to let go of in order for this group to flourish?" There are many things we carry that can get in the way of a group. It could be certainty, self-righteousness or rigid positions. It could be our unwillingness to contribute, or our need to control the process too tightly. When each of us is accountable for confronting our own learning edges and for making changes in ourselves, the flow of the entire group can open up.

The second question is, "What do I need from the group in order to show up fully with all my gifts, talents, and ideas?" Sometimes we adjust to group dynamics by withdrawing from the discussion and just silently observing the group. This prevents us from contributing our wisdom to the group's work. The very thing the group most needs may be our contribution. If we remind ourselves that what we have to offer is indeed needed, we can more easily find it within ourselves to ask the group to support us in ways that enable us to contribute fully.

❖   **Dimension 4: Learn as a group.** Groups that know how to learn together can adapt to almost any challenge. This is not an easy process for many of us. Learning together involves making explicit the sticky issues in the group or the work and working through the stuck places.

Some groups do this work together. A local branch of a political party wanted to create a different kind of conversation about public issues — one that moved from debate toward a more positive dialogue on issues. They created a rule that modeled this approach. The rule was: if you have an issue, we need to handle it in public. This created a transparency that allowed them to shift to more positive public dialogues.

In other groups, people discuss challenging issues privately. An issue may arise between several people in the group, but individuals can feel too vulnerable handling it publicly in the large group, so they take it off-line. Once they work through the issue in the subgroup, it helps tremendously to bring the learning back to the large group. Not only does this resolve questions or misinformation that may have arisen when the small group broke off, but the whole group can benefit from what the subgroup learned.

When learning in public, we need to become more comfortable with our discomfort. If we try too quickly to prevent or eliminate discomfort from our processes, we will keep the group from developing more powerful relationships. We need to be able to create openings for participants to say what needs to be said even if it produces discomfort. Much of learning theory is based on the tension between two concepts: challenge and support. If there is to be development, a certain amount of challenge is necessary. And similarly, we need enough support so challenges do not overwhelm us. Gracious Space brings this balance when learning in public.

Assessing Competency in the Four Elements

Change agents will benefit from assessing their own grasp of the four elements. People who have been practicing Gracious Space for any length of time develop a comfort level with some or all of the four elements. Some people may feel very comfortable with one of the elements, and less comfortable with the others, necessitating their constant attention and practice. We have noticed that there are two primary ways people engage with the four elements. Some feel they can *be* Gracious Space quite naturally, that the approach of Gracious Space is innate and they can embody the concepts easily and effortlessly. Other people feel more comfortable *doing* Gracious Space. They prefer to rely on a large and tested kit of activities and exercises to help activate the elements of Gracious Space in groups.

In either example, people who feel more comfortable with one aspect often feel a gap in the other. Consequently they seek handholds to build their competence in their area of discomfort. The Center wants to assist people in developing a high degree of competency and readiness to both *be* and *do* Gracious Space.

The first step to creating Gracious Space in a group is to determine which of the four elements the group needs to attend to most. Does the group need to identify and claim individual gifts and spirit? Is the setting appropriate to the type of conversation or change process? Are the 'strangers' voices represented and being heard? Is the group willing and capable of learning together over time? The assessment of the presence and strength of the four elements will begin to form and strengthen the container for change.

Following this chapter is a Personal Competency Worksheet, designed to assess your level of competence in carrying out each of the four elements. We encourage you to think about both the attitudes and approaches (being) and the tools and activities (doing) that you already know and use, and then brainstorm to discover how you can bring Gracious Space to life. There is also a Gracious Space Self-Assessment following this chapter, offered to help you identify which characteristics of Gracious Space you naturally possess and which you may want to develop. Thirdly, there is a Group Competency Assessment to help you think about how the group is doing with respect to its understanding and practice of Gracious Space.

These tools form the beginning of the Practitioner's Workspace, a set of reflective and diagnostic questions and activities which will follow each chapter in Part One.

Gracious Space Practitioner Workspace
Assessing Personal Competency

Each quadrant in the circle below represents one of the four elements of Gracious Space.

Each element has three levels:
Novice: center of the circle   Proficient: at the hash mark   Master: on the circle

Assess your capacity for being Gracious Space (carrying the inner attitude and readiness) in working with each element, and place a mark at your current capacity.

Assess your capacity for doing Gracious Space (having a tool kit and activities) for each element, and place a mark at your current capacity.

In each quadrant, note the ways and behaviors of being and the tools and activities for doing you already know and use to activate the element.

Connect the marks to get a visual representation of your current competency.

Each quadrant in the circle below represents one of the four elements of Gracious Space.

Each element has three levels:
Novice: center of the circle   Proficient: at the hash mark   Master: on the circle

Assess your *group's* capacity for being Gracious Space (carrying the inner attitude and readiness) in working with each element, and place a mark at your current capacity.

Assess your *group's* capacity for doing Gracious Space (having a tool kit and activities) for each element, and place a mark at your current capacity.

In each quadrant, note the ways and behaviors of being and the tools and activities for doing the group already knows and uses to activate the element.

Connect the marks to get a visual representation of the group's current competency.

Gracious Space Practitioner Workspace
Self-Assessment

Gracious Space: A spirit and setting where we invite the 'stranger' and learn in public.

Instructions: Below is a list of values and behaviors that can demonstrate Gracious Space. Check all those you feel describe you. Then *circle* the top three that truly define the spirit you carry with you.

1_____   2_____   3_____

Star two areas where you would like to improve.

1_____   2_____

- Establishing norms
- Interjecting humor/fun
- Affirming others
- Being open to feedback
- Accepting of different perspectives and ideas
- Innovating new approaches
- Being present
- Being aware of my impact on others
- Assuming others' best intentions
- Being intentional
- Being reliable
- Trusting others
- Being trustworthy
- Willing to change my mind
- Willing to slow down

- Reflecting on assumptions
- Actively seek others' opinions
- Being curious
- Asking open-ended questions
- Discerning patterns emerging from a group discussion
- Learning and sharing rather than just advocating
- Listening deeply and generatively
- Willing to be influenced
- Being comfortable receiving lots of questions
- Being comfortable not knowing
- Able to detach from outcomes
- Being collaborative
- Capable of stopping, reassessing and redirecting

- Fascinated/curious about differences
- Being open to differing and conflicting views
- Welcoming others not in my comfort zone
- Being compassionate
- Empowering others
- Being authentic
- Feeling comfortable with community wisdom
- Building community
- Bridging boundaries
- Extending respect to everyone
- Sharing power
- Seeing everyone as gifted and capable
- Holding off on judgment
- Steering conflict toward positive, creative results

Stepping Into
the Field of Change

"Be the change you want to see in the world."
—Mahatma Gandhi

Before proceeding with an in-depth exploration of the Gracious Space Change Framework, we would like to share what we have discovered about change processes in general. By becoming aware of the dynamics that characterize most change processes, it becomes easy to understand how the Gracious Space Framework can be so effective.

People seek change because of their desire to make things better. We all carry ideas about what makes change happen and what will create the outcomes we desire. These ideas inform our behavior, often at a subconscious level. There are many theories and models that explain how to think about, plan for and engage change. These theories help us reflect on our experiences and consider what worked, why our actions may or may not have produced the results we hoped for, and what to do differently.

When we first began to develop the Gracious Space Change Framework, we reviewed our favorite change models. We also reviewed change processes we had participated in and analyzed how the elements of Gracious Space contributed to their success. Examples ranged from creating a more welcoming environment at a childcare center to leading a complex change process with thousands of citizens in neighborhood planning for the City of Seattle.

As we reviewed these various approaches, we recognized that the elements of Gracious Space were integral to all of them, provided that people cared about each other and wanted to be involved in something that served a goal greater than limited self-interest. Even though everyone involved in a change process wanted something better for their community or organization, or wanted something better than the change process they were currently working with, we found that everyone had varying capacities to engage in the change process and differing interpretations of what was needed.

We also noticed that when people paid attention to the elements of Gracious Space — spirit, setting, invite the 'stranger,' and learn in public — in order to intentionally improve how they learned from each other and worked together, they were more likely to open up to transformative change. This was true even if people were calling what they did by something other than Gracious Space.

Known and Unknown

The common denominator of all of the change theories we reviewed is that people are working with what they know while dealing with what they don't know. Change theories offer a way to claim what we know (or believe we know) in order to make sense of a broader context and to guide decisions about how we act. In any moment, some parts are known to us, and others are not. Our personal response to the known and unknown influence how we approach change. If we think we already know all the answers, then we have quit learning — at least until the unknown informs us, sometimes in dramatic ways, that there is more to learn.

What we mean by "known" begins with the belief that what has worked before will work again. In known territory, we are confident that we understand the people involved, what they need, how they think and are likely to respond. We believe that the processes that have produced good results in the past will continue to produce good results. We are convinced that underlying conditions are stable and the major influences at play will be similar in the future. Many change initiatives start with logic models that describe what participants will do to achieve a particular outcome. Logic models clarify our assumptions about which activities make a difference so we can focus our actions toward better results. This approach assumes that the past is, for the most part, an accurate predictor of the future.

There is another kind of knowing which taps into the deep truths that guide us. A Native American community we worked with in New Mexico is committed to the truths that have guided them for over a thousand years. For this community, change involves understanding how those deep truths shape and inform the current environment. Any change process that seeks to alter the community's relationship to those deep truths has little resonance. Based in these truths, their leadership approach is about being of service to the whole community, and any form of leadership that elevates the individual above the community is not welcome. These are people who know what matters to them and are clear about staying in that knowing.

Another way of describing this deep knowing is provided by Michael Meade in his book, <u>World Behind the World</u>. Meade talks about deep truths that persist regardless of what is happening on the day-to-day surface of events, even cataclysmic ones. These truths continue to exist, even as the daily world shifts or unravels. For example, the importance of family guides our choices even as our assumptions about what family or marriage means and who is part of it may be being redefined by the culture. These deep truths knit the world together in surprising ways.

For many of us, however, acting on the known is not as much about these deep truths. It is more about finding a way to make the day-to-day events of our lives predictable enough to allow us to live in safe, comfortable and productive ways.

When we speak of the "unknown," we mean that circumstances are changing so rapidly that we question whether what has worked in the past is likely to work in the future. Or, we are engaged with people who see the world in fundamentally different ways, and we are not sure we understand those ways or even how to begin effective communications to understand each other better. Or, we are launching a new project, program, or service that is different from anything we have done before. One of the new terms for describing our current work and social environments is VUCA: volatile, uncertain, complex and ambiguous. The emergence of this term speaks to the ubiquitous level of the unknown in our fast changing world. In these cases, we need to explore the unknown in order to find a better way to make change.

One person who is willing to work in this territory is C. Otto Scharmer, a Massachusetts Institute of Technology economist. He offers a methodology to "presence the future" in order to develop new approaches that move away from the failures of the past. Inherent in this approach is a healthy skepticism that acting on what we know from the past will produce anything different from what we already have. In his process, a change agent opens up to the deepest level of who he or she is in order to create a shift and make a difference.

For obvious reasons, many of us are much more comfortable with the known. We want to make sure that most, if not all, of our work is in known territory because the alternative seems too scary. We fear that the unknown will move us out of our comfortable places, perhaps into danger. We believe that if we fortify against uncertainty and increase our control we can make things more predictable. A person's reflexive response to encountering the unknown clearly influences and affects whether change will be embraced or resisted.

This is where Gracious Space comes in. If our change processes are to be effective, we have to be able to stand in VUCA conditions and not shut down. We have to learn how to be comfortable in uncomfortable situations and trust that we will all be fine. Gracious Space helps us in these emergent and adaptive environments because it enables us to hear new information, learn in public about surprises and uncertainties, and develop the relationships and strategies to run toward the roar. The more we consciously practice Gracious Space, the more experience we have with seeking out new ideas that challenge us. The more we learn in public when confronted with our own limitations, the more chance we have of not getting lost when confusion arises.

Gracious Space is a catalyst that transforms our fixed, rigid perceptions into more flexible and evolution-friendly ones. This is at the heart of inviting the 'stranger' and strange ideas. Practicing Gracious Space invites us to see the unknown as an opportunity to learn and grow. This helps us run toward the roar.

Surprise

Surprise can be seen as the marker between the known and the unknown. Understanding how we view surprise and how we respond when we are surprised helps us consider what it takes to stay open to learning in public — a key component of Gracious Space.

Charles Darwin, the father of evolution theory, was said to carry a notebook with him so he could record surprises when he encountered them. He wrote his observations in this notebook, since his experience told him that otherwise he would not be able to remember what he had seen. His mind (like ours) had no place to store a fact that didn't fit into his current, overall understanding of how the world works.

In <u>Mistakes Were Made (but not by me)</u>, Carol Tavris and Elliot Aronson describe the incredible ability we have as human beings to limit what we see and to remake our memories so that all of the information we have access to supports what we already "know" to be true. They note that we have to be ever vigilant because individuals, groups, and institutions do everything we can to reduce dissonance, which, if acknowledged, would get in the way of maintaining business as usual. It is easy to frame surprises as errors, mistakes or irrelevancies, even to the point of forgetting what was surprising. This, of course, reduces our ability to learn from our new experiences.

When working in different government agencies, we often heard managers give this instruction to staff: "I don't want any surprises." This primarily referred to the manager's strong wish to learn about a major problem from staff rather than from the press or the City Council. However, this statement, which is not unique to government, reflects a deeper belief — namely, that good management means having enough information and skill to keep bad things from happening. Often we assume that surprise means something has "gone wrong." We think surprises mean that someone has made a mistake that could have been prevented — if only someone had been more vigilant, or caution had been better exercised, or something had been done better.

In our highly litigious society, we "know" that someone or something else is to blame for almost anything that has undesirable consequences. In these circumstances, we use surprise as an indicator of our failure to know enough. And, we somehow imagine that the proper response to this failing is to develop ways of gathering more information so that we are better prepared for similar situations in the future. Unfortunately, when we see surprise as something that is undesirable and wrong, our potential to see the vast majority of the world whose door is opened by surprise is greatly diminished. We lose access to the realm of an unfolding universe that is moving forward in a way that is beyond our analytical ability to anticipate.

Rueben Daniels wrote an article titled "Surprise, Surprise, Surprise! A Complexity Science View of the Unexpected," which offered an alternate way of viewing surprise. He notes that most often surprise is viewed as a threat, or an error based in ignorance. However, in complex systems, surprise is inevitable because it is part of the natural order of things and cannot be avoided, eliminated or controlled. Complex systems are emergent realities, which have many parts interacting in nonlinear ways. Sometimes what is happening is simply unknowable and unpredictable because it is emerging in the moment and is new and different from previous experiences. From this perspective, surprise is a gift. It is an early indicator that things are not working as we think they should, or imagined they would, based on the given set of assumptions we happen to be carrying.

If we can embrace surprise as an early sign that the patterns we are familiar with are changing, then we have time to adapt and respond in ways that are more creative and innovative. Welcoming surprise opens up a completely different field of possibilities. This includes working with the surprise and building on what has unexpectedly happened to get where we still want to go, but now in a different way. It also demands a different level of personal awareness in order for us to notice what is actually happening rather than what we think should be happening. And, it demands personal alertness and accountability to remain in a creative and possible frame of mind rather than shutting down when the unexpected arrives. It might be helpful to keep track of surprises in a notebook like Darwin did, in order to discern a helpful pattern that could inform our work.

In quickly changing environments, it is critical to be open to learning in public. If everyone shares what they are seeing and what is surprising them, the group as a whole has more intelligence at hand when making decisions about what to do next. Often this requires leveling the power dynamics so that everyone can offer their gifts and perspectives with greater confidence and ease. As we move into the Gracious Space Change Framework, we will share some methods that support leveling power dynamics and inviting the 'stranger.' Acknowledging that everyone has a perspective that is important to the issue is very much about being open to surprise.

Sometimes, people on the so-called "fringe" of the system can see what is going on and what is possible in ways that people in the center cannot. Sometimes, when people have been trained to see the presupposed known as the only way things can work, they are not able to discern the clues that major change is desirable and on its way.

The history of technological change is full of examples of businesses so immersed in their own way of thinking that they missed the wave of the next evolution — e.g., Swiss watch makers who missed digital watches; IBM, which missed personal computers; and Microsoft, which almost missed the internet. A great story comes from the world of physics. In 1900, Lord Kelvin famously stated, "There is nothing new to be discovered in physics now. All that remains is more and more precise measurement." Five years later, Albert Einstein published his paper on special relativity, challenging the rules of Newtonian mechanics, which had been used to describe force and motion for over two hundred years.

For many of us the most challenging time to openheartedly embrace change is when much of what we know, and have come to rely on, is put in question — when systems are in transition and/or collapsing and the next configuration is not yet clear. If we are relatively comfortable in the place we are in, it can be hard to embrace the notion that the next configuration will be as good or better. The following story from a colleague illustrates the power of the known:

"In my first job as supervisor, I held interviews with each staff person, during which they disclosed a high level of frustration with their jobs and the work environment. I spent a year improving systems and moving people to try new positions. Then I announced that we would develop a new organizational plan together. Naively, I thought people would be eager to stabilize after a year of transitions and would embrace the process since they would be proactively involved.

Instead, they went to the union to block any change. I felt betrayed. How could they not see the great new future I was inviting them to help create? A key lesson from this experience was to not underestimate the powerful comfort of what is known, even when it is hated. Once I understood how fearful my staff was of change, we were able to construct a gentler process that led to an improved structure."

Fear, anger and other strong emotions triggered by stress often activate reactions from the limbic (animal) brain that generate fight or flight behaviors. On the other hand, positive imagination and creativity come from the neo-cortex that, unfortunately, shuts down (by being deprived of blood) when the limbic part of the brain takes over. If we cannot face our fears and move through them, we physiologically and practically diminish our capacity to find satisfying, innovative alternatives to address the challenges in front of us. When we engage in Gracious Space, we increase our collective capacity to turn fear of the unknown into the love of possibility. Gracious Space is a practice ground for learning in public. It is a place where our fear of failing or falling short diminishes.

In our culture we have long equated being a leader with having the answer or knowing what direction should be taken. The lessons of Gracious Space show otherwise. Being a leader means being comfortable with not knowing in order to find something better. One manager described her move from the traditional viewpoint to one that embraces learning in public:

> *"When someone asked me a question, I thought I should be able to respond and provide appropriate direction. That made me very fearful of what I did not know and fearful that people would find out how much I needed to learn. Once I let go of the notion that leadership was about knowing the answers, and once I saw that leadership was really about asking the right questions, I felt liberated! It meant that instead of finding the answer (or making one up), I could find out whether there was someone in the room who actually knew what was needed. Using Gracious Space opened up the possibility that someone else would take ownership for finding a better answer."*

Knowing that others are with us in the work and that their insights and gifts contribute to how we move forward creates more capacity to be together in the unknown. Standing in the questions that need to be explored opens us to the power of surprise. Instead of inflicting upon ourselves rigid, destination-driven efforts aimed at controlling the unknown, we open to an ongoing journey where specific destinations are markers on the path, not ends in themselves. The more answers we find, the more questions we generate. And as we become practiced in this new approach, the realization that we will never have all the answers ceases to feel overwhelming.

Summary

The role of Gracious Space in transformative change is clear. When we collectively pay attention to the spirit and setting in which we open to learning together and when we welcome insights from people whom we hadn't previously considered asking, we increase the potential for more creativity and innovation. Gracious Space helps us to create the conditions for transformative change in which we confront the unknown in ourselves as well as that in the external world.

Following this chapter is a worksheet to help change agents reflect on personal change-related situations, name the known and unknown elements, and assess their emotional responses. It is important to name a specific context, not only because the known and unknown will be different in each one, but also because the emotional reaction is often different in different parts of our lives.

Briefly describe your change project or process:

In the boxes below, reflect on the aspects of your change initiative that are known or unknown.

	KNOWN	UNKNOWN
Clarity of purpose — *shared sense among participants of why it matters and what people value in the work*		
Context — *history, power dynamics, heritage, what needs to heal, culture of place and group*		
People — *who is involved, types of relationships, gifts of those involved, expectations*		
Agreements — *on what needs to be done, how it needs to be done, who will do it*		
Environment — *funding, what is happening around the change that will impact it, predictability of conditions*		

Personal Reflection:

When you review how you have filled in this page, what do you feel? Write or draw what you are feeling.

Where is your comfort zone relative to working with known conditions and unknown conditions?

What happens to you when you get outside your comfort zone?

Are your core strengths a better match for situations when the territory is known or when it is unknown; or do they work in both territories?

How can you develop capacity in your less comfortable zone?

Chapter Three

An Overview of the Gracious Space Change Framework

"Things should be as simple as possible, but not simpler."
— Albert Einstein

Gracious Space is a dynamic container for change, a crucible into which we can put our most pressing conflict, culture change, strategic planning process or other dynamic change process. The first Gracious Space book described the four core elements — spirit, setting, invite the 'stranger' and learn in public — as related but separate entities. Now we put them together in a dynamic way to form the framework for change that this book is about. The Gracious Space Change Framework enables change agents and groups to apply the transformative insights and processes of Gracious Space to their change efforts.

We have identified four key components that affect the change process: the energetic state of the group, the concrete actions of the group, the inner life of the change agent and the inner life of the group as an entity. The Framework explores the interplay of these components with each other and within the context of the four elements of Gracious Space. This overview is intended to give the reader a snapshot of the Gracious Space Change Framework and its potential. The following chapters delve more deeply into all aspects of the Framework.

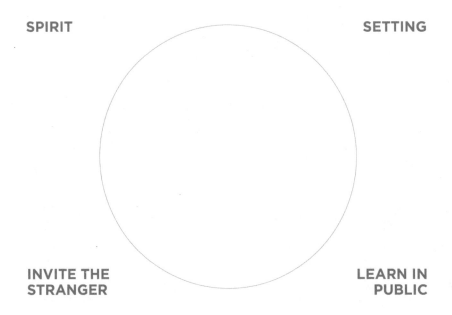

Creating the Container

SPIRIT   SETTING

INVITE THE   LEARN IN
STRANGER   PUBLIC

Creating the Container

The four core elements of Gracious Space serve as the container, depicted as a circle (above) to represent wholeness. It is within the container of the four elements that the work of the Framework takes place. In our model, the change agent uses the four elements of Gracious Space as a lens to better understand the workings of the change process, as a diagnostic tool to figure out what is working and not working within that change process and, finally, as a set of strategies to remedy the problems once they are known and to move the process into new realms of possibility.

To create the container within which all the work gets done, we need to pay attention to all four elements, but particularly, to which one(s) the group needs most at the moment. Does the group need to identify and claim individual gifts and spirit? Is the setting appropriate to the type of conversation or change process the group wishes to engage in? Is the 'stranger's' voice represented and heard? Is the group willing and capable of learning together over time? An assessment of the strength of the four elements starts to shape the container which will hold the change work. Once the container is created, groups can explore the key components of change, including the emotional and concrete sides of change as well as the inner life of the change agent and the inner work of the group.

Working Together

The Four Openings

Inside the container is the soft "V" shape that describes the working together part of the Change Framework (shown below). On the left side are the Four Openings groups experience as part of this change process: Opening to Safety, Opening to Relationship, Opening to Risk and Opening to Collective Creativity. These are the *energetic states of a*

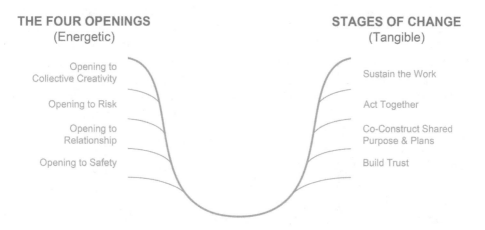

The Four Openings
The Four Stages of Change

THE FOUR OPENINGS
(Energetic)

STAGES OF CHANGE
(Tangible)

Opening to
Collective Creativity

Opening to Risk

Opening to
Relationship

Opening to Safety

Sustain the Work

Act Together

Co-Construct Shared
Purpose & Plans

Build Trust

group as it advances in its ability to listen more, judge less, hold uncertainty and lean into possibility. By energetic, we mean groups possess a certain energy during the change process. If the energy is tight, competitive, fearful or restrictive — like the energy we get holding a closed fist — there is less opening and less likelihood change will be successful. If the energy is relaxed, available, open or willing — like the energy we feel holding our hands open in front of us — there is more opening and more likelihood that collaborative change will be successful.

❖   **Opening to Safety.** Safety is created by making things known: who is here, what they want, how the process works, what can be expected, what each person's role is, etc. Without safety, a group will stall at the very beginning. When we wish to encourage people to show up and bring their ideas to the table without judgment, shaming or violence, we focus on creating safety. This opening supports buy-in for the change effort.

❖   **Opening to Relationship.** Relationships are the vehicle by which work gets done, and strong relationships make the change work more likely to succeed. Strengthening relationships helps establish greater predictability and understanding, while simultaneously freeing members to bring their gifts and contributions. The focus is on group members interacting, learning to trust and work together, and jointly defining the work that needs to be done.

❖   **Opening to Risk.** Many groups create safety and relationship but then fail to face the discomfort, conflict or paradoxical nature of their work because they are not willing to risk the safety and relationship they have created. In change work true safety often eludes us until we face that which makes us fearful. Sometimes our well-intentioned actions or beliefs actually prevent us from getting where we want to be. To move from being stuck to a more powerful place, groups need to open to risk, face discomfort and explore the truth from multiple viewing points. This results in breakthrough thinking, which is not possible when the group stays on a superficial level of safety and agreement.

❖   **Opening to Collective Creativity.** At this stage the group is willing and able to be in an extended state of "not knowing." They are open to uncertainty and new possibilities. Together they create something unexpected and more powerful than previously dreamed. In this state, the group co-constructs the whole, and then determines the parts and assignments that flow out of it.

We recognize that in change processes occurring in emergent environments, no process is linear. Groups will experience all of the openings simultaneously to some degree. However, this Framework indicates a sequential progression that we believe will yield the greatest benefits. Successful groups should attempt to accomplish the earlier openings to be ready for those that follow. A foundation of safety will yield better relationships and a greater capacity to risk and be creative in new territory. Often, groups want to plunge in at the Opening of Collective Creativity. They may be excited or under pressure to generate results and therefore desire to be at a high level of performance. But if they haven't deliberately ventured into the Openings of Safety, Relationship and Risk, the creative work can become mired in conflict, apathy and frustration. The group wonders what went wrong, and then (hopefully) realizes they must back up to develop more safety, relationship and capacity to engage with risk.

The Four Stages of Change

On the right side of the Framework are the Four Stages of Change: Build Trust, Co-Construct Shared Purpose and Plans, Act Together, and Sustain the Work. These are the *tangible and concrete actions* groups take to advance the change process. This work yields visible, tangible progress: meetings get called; people join; decisions get made; mission statements are agreed upon; work assignments are made; timelines are formed; work gets done. Like the Four Openings, the Four Stages of Change also progress in a sequential way. Simply stated, actions will be superior if trust is built and purposes and plans are co-constructed before the action is implemented.

Our experience has shown that most groups focus on this component of the change work at the expense of all the others, because they want to jump straight to action. One of the unique qualities of the Gracious Space Change Framework is that it pairs the concrete stages of change with the Four Openings. For example, in order to build trust, we must create safety. In order to co-construct shared plans and purpose, we must develop strong relationships. The Gracious Space Change Framework pairs the Openings and the Stages of Change to illuminate the integral nature of change work.

❖   **Build Trust.** The group gets to know each other and identifies culture, history, strengths and challenges. Individuals share their values, gifts, resources, capacities and passions. The group agrees how to work together while honoring differences.

❖   **Co-Construct Shared Purpose and Plans.** Since this is a collaborative model, the group together develops the shared purpose and roadmap to advance their change work. This stage is not done by a leadership team or sub-group and then handed off to others as a stone tablet, rather the group as a whole takes responsibility for the shared purpose that can hold individual passions and gifts.

❖   **Act Together.** Sub-groups take on assignments, keeping their work in alignment with the larger vision. The group holds each other accountable for the commitments they make to stay engaged and to continue learning. They implement the plan, adapting as needed, and build allies who can act in concert with the shared purpose.

❖   **Sustain the Change Work.** The changes, both internal and external, become a way of life that deepens over time. The group creates the means and structures to keep people engaged and to welcome new partners. They adapt the work as they learn more about what works and what is needed.

The Inner Work

In the center of the Framework is the infinity sign, or a Möbius Strip, that represents the inner journey of the individual and the inner life of the group. A Möbius Strip has only one side; it is created by taking a thin length of paper and making one twist, then taping the ends together. If an ant traveled along the strip it would walk on both sides and return to the starting point without ever crossing an edge. The two "sides" of the strip represent the distinct but connected and mutually reinforcing aspects of the inner life of change work. Both individuals and groups must attend to their patterns to identify and transform limits to learning and growth.

Practice of the Change Agent

The change agent is always part of the change, and the inner life of the change agent has an impact on the quality of the change itself. Change agents must pay attention to the spirit we bring, our preparation, our intentions, where our attention lies, our comfort zone in the context of change, assumptions about group patterns and our ability to facilitate within that comfort or discomfort. The slightest change in how we think about someone or something will have an impact. What might we need to attend to be of better service to the group or the issue?

Masterful change agency is an ongoing dance of skill, presence and inspiration. Outwardly the change agent's role is to help participants move through the agenda in accordance with the purpose, principles and articulated norms for working together. Inwardly, we remain centered and authentic, attentive to what is emerging, inviting

The Inner Work

**PRACTICE
OF THE
CHANGE AGENT**

**WORK OF THE
GROUP**

the group to move to a new stage of openness, standing in creative tension and ready to shift in a moment to best serve the group. Change agents need to have a personal practice that builds their own capacity to remain centered and authentic in the midst of dynamic, emergent change. How do we make the personal shifts that make transformational change more likely to occur?

Work of the Group

Just as change agents must attend to their own practice, a group working for change must attend to its inner life. Too often groups focus on task or the "what" of change, at the expense of their own process, or the "how" of change. The Gracious Space Change Framework illuminates the relational field of a group, how to identify common group patterns, reinforce positive patterns, and shift patterns that cause groups to be stuck. The group notices what it must let go in order to be of better service to the change effort.

The group needs to remain open and ever-conscious of patterns and learning that are emerging. Holding ambiguity, questioning assumptions, making the implicit explicit, naming the "elephant in the room," illuminating patterns, and identifying breakthroughs are all skill sets that group work can develop. The process reshapes itself to hold the conversation that is ready and most needed to happen. The group pays attention to shifts in energy, disturbances and conflict, new flow after stuckness, moments of reflection to gather insights and opportunities for a transformative move.

A Capacity Building Framework

One of the notable characteristics of the Gracious Space Change Framework is that it embraces change from the inside out. Who we are as individuals and groups has everything to do with how successful our change work will be. We stand firmly in the belief that the work we do to be our best is an integral part of any change effort to make the world a better place.

The Gracious Space Change Framework is also a capacity building model because, as we work within the model — building safety and trust, developing strong relationships, exploring the inner life of the self and group, and co-constructing purpose with people who share our passion and with whom we creatively act together — we develop our personal and group capacity for doing that exact same work, only better, next time around.

Once we build these capacities, we get to keep them. Like a child who develops the capacity for language, we own it forever. This is good news for the Gracious Space practitioner! Once we learn how to embody safety, build trust and develop strong relationships with others, we can draw on those capacities in the future. Once we know how to navigate risk and collective creativity and act together to implement and sustain our good work, we can tap these capacities each time

Gracious Space Change Framework

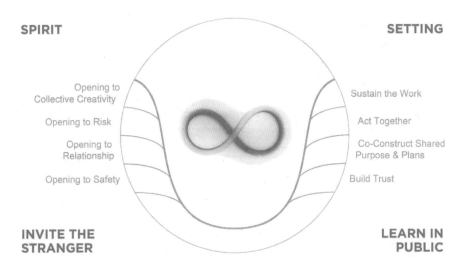

SPIRIT

SETTING

Opening to
Collective Creativity

Sustain the Work

Opening to Risk

Act Together

Opening to
Relationship

Co-Construct Shared
Purpose & Plans

Opening to Safety

Build Trust

INVITE THE
STRANGER

LEARN IN
PUBLIC

we engage in new ventures. When we explore our own practices and understand the patterns of groups, that wisdom comes with us to the next situation. Access to those capacities is established, we know how it feels when we are there, and we know how to relate to others in that place.

Fortunately or unfortunately, we are always working in new settings, new processes or with new people. This means that even though we may have built our own capacity and that of the group we worked with, we have to begin again with the Openings and Stages with the new folks. We can't just jump in at the previous high level of functioning we have enjoyed. We need to bring our cumulatively learned knowledge and apply it afresh with the new group. If a core team forms and builds trust in the co-construction of shared purpose, this same trust building work will be required when the group expands, although the time can be shortened and the ideas will be fed by work already completed.

We experienced this phenomenon repeatedly in the Kellogg Leadership for Community Change program. After working together for a year or two, a group of leaders inevitably developed a high degree of capacity. But when they brought in new people, or invited the 'stranger' so they could expand the project to a larger segment of the community, they found they had to begin again with this larger group.

This is often a source of frustration, especially for those who have experienced a peak performance with a team in the past. They want to be at a high level of performance quickly, and may grow impatient or frustrated when they are not, and even resist efforts at safety and relationship building, thinking them superfluous. Everyone wants to start at the level of collective creativity or begin acting together immediately. But if the group has not developed the individual and shared capacity for safety, trust, relationships and working through risk, how much breakthrough thinking are they really going to achieve?

The Framework is also a capacity building model in that as we navigate within the core elements, the Four Openings, the Four Stages of Change and the Inner Work of change, the container itself becomes more resilient and capable of holding the dynamics of change. As we activate the various components and elements of the model, we weave them together. The action of moving back and forth between the aspects of the model, much like weaving a tapestry or a basket, creates form and strength. Yet the weaving does not result in a constrictive container, but rather a more expansive one. Weaving produces the ability to hold more, thereby offering greater capacity to hold increasingly more complex change work.

Perhaps an image will demonstrate this more clearly. Imagine that we start engaging with the Change Framework at a particular opening, for example, Opening to Safety. When we enter from this place, and then pair that with building trust or another component of the framework, we discover new possibilities for ourselves, the group and the change work. It is as if we enter the container through an opening or stage and discover a whole cosmos inside full of possibility. The possibilities are held inside, and the more energy that is brought to the work, the more we gain access to those possibilities and the more capable the container becomes to hold the dynamics of change.

At one of our Gracious Space trainings, a participant shared a piece of art that depicted his understanding of Gracious Space. It was a round pottery vase with a painting of a ladder leading to a decorative opening carved into one of the sides. The internal walls were painted dark blue and covered with stars and constellations. Inside the container was not emptiness, nor a constricted space, but the universe of possibility!

Extending the imagery further, imagine that a hole is poked in the bottom of the container. The energy will swirl downwards and drain out. Gossip, aggression, dishonesty, retribution, control — these are some behaviors which threaten the heart of our work and form holes in the container. Engaging in and sustaining behaviors that build rather than drain will reinforce the capacity building ability of the container.

It is also important to remember that although represented linearly, this Framework is actually cyclical. We are never done with safety and building trust; relationships can always be stronger; the seeds of collective creativity and sustainability are sown from the first moment of gathering. At any step in the change process groups may need to revisit one of the earlier Openings or Stages. Thinking of the Openings and Stages as spirals reminds us that when we come around to a particular spot again, the experience will be shaped by what happened before, and groups will deepen their understanding of how best to do their work each time they revisit a particular Opening or Stage. As the change spirals up into new experiences of inclusivity, capacity and possibility, the group will require more trust-building and re-shaping of the purpose, which reflects broadened interests.

Summary

The Gracious Space Change Framework is a dynamic container and capacity-building model for complex change processes. It enables change agents and groups to apply the transformative insights and processes of Gracious Space to their change efforts. Using the Framework generates learning and change from the inside out, and guides people to create safety, build trust, form relationships, construct shared plans and purpose, take risks, take action together, sustain their collective creativity and explore the inner life of the change agent and the group. The Framework is intended to support courageously collaborative efforts to build lasting and positive change in service to all. The Framework is intended to expand what's possible.

Chapter Four

The Four Openings

"If you want to go fast, go alone. If you want to go far, go together."

— *African proverb*

As a catalyst and container for collaborative change, Gracious Space is both relationship- and outcome-oriented. When we say Gracious Space is relationship-oriented, we mean that it is largely by and through relationships that change occurs. In this chapter, we explore the relational aspects of the Gracious Space Change Framework that drive how we are together in the work.

Most of what we aspire to do in our lives involves other people — whether at work, at home, or in community. Today's scientists and business gurus say that it is by and through people that breakthrough, innovation and good work happens, not through spreadsheets, financial reports and strategic plans. We need each other to get things done. We need each other to understand who we are, what we are capable of, and to accomplish our dreams. From the microscopic to the global, systems are relational and interconnected. Physicist and systems theorist Fritjof Capra is quoted in <u>Presence</u>, as saying: "At all levels of life, from the metabolic networks inside cells to the food webs of ecosystems and the networks of communications in human societies, the components of living systems are inter-linked in network fashion."

Yet in our human interactions, we often struggle with unhelpful and harmful means of interaction — debate, shouting opinions at each other, polite civility, over-managing each other, selling partial answers versus seeking solutions, working around each other, refusing to acknowledge the truth in what another person says, refusing to share power — none of which advance us toward desired outcomes. We often get in our own way and thwart the results we most desire.

Most people want something different. We want to open up to new possibilities. We want to feel safer, develop deeper relationships, bridge boundaries that separate us and create greater possibilities for working together. "Because [we become] embedded in a system of social relations that keeps getting more complex — this normally starts in early childhood and then goes on later in life — the most important decisions a human being can make in the course of his life are psycho-social in nature," says Gerald Heuther in <u>The Compassionate Brain</u>.

By paying attention to the energetic Four Openings, we can help our groups be ready for the change work and be prepared to stay in it once engaged. By paying attention to these openings, the group will begin to make the unknown, known. They will feel safer, develop stronger relationships, be more willing and able to step into risk, and lean into collective creativity. These are not necessarily things the group *does*; rather, these are attitudes or postures we *embody* while doing the change work.

In this chapter we will explain the Four Openings and why they matter, different qualities to pay attention to, how to engage in them, what blocks the openings and knowing how and when to move forward.

The Four Openings
The Four Stages of Change

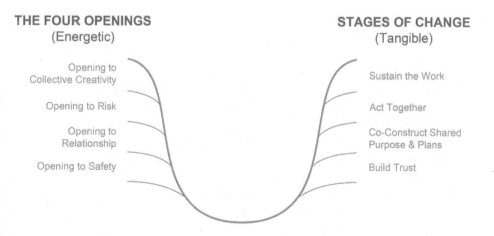

THE FOUR OPENINGS (Energetic)	STAGES OF CHANGE (Tangible)
Opening to Collective Creativity	Sustain the Work
Opening to Risk	Act Together
Opening to Relationship	Co-Construct Shared Purpose & Plans
Opening to Safety	Build Trust

Opening to Safety

What is safety and why does it matter? Safety is the feeling of being free, comfortable and unthreatened in being oneself. Maslow's Hierarchy of Needs describes safety as a foundation of human development. At the bottom of Maslow's pyramid are physiological needs, such as breathing, food, water and sleep. The next level is about safety, which Maslow defines as security of body, employment, resources, morality, family, health and property. Meeting these needs satisfactorily frees up the individual to focus on the more complex aspects of life, including love and belonging, esteem, and self-actualization. Without safety, attaining any kind of collective change built on meaningful engagement will be difficult if not impossible.

Safety is primarily created by doing two things: eliminating unknowns and building trust. In Opening to Safety we are attempting to bring in more of the known so people can relax. Remember: if people are afraid, they will shut down. We also should remember that some people may feel safe in circumstances that are risky and others won't feel safe no matter what is going on. Oftentimes, we don't necessarily create safety; we help people find it in themselves.

Ways to help people find their sense of safety include making known the names of everyone in the room, the purpose of the work, how the process works, unique terminology, what can be expected, each person's role, the timeframe, hoped-for outcomes, and potential hazards or hurdles. At this stage we want to gently invite people to engage in minimal risk activities. For some, just saying their name in public is a challenge! Creating a safe space is a critical step that we cannot skip.

We typically focus on Opening to Safety at the beginning of a change effort, when we wish to encourage people to show up and bring their ideas to the table without judgment, shame, blame or violence. The focus is on inviting authentic interest and inclusion for the change effort. We know how a safe space feels. We know it changes the interaction. In safety we feel secure to speak our mind, raise questions and be vulnerable with others yet feel supported, trusting that our words or actions will not be misinterpreted or used against us in the future. Safety is a peaceful, expansive feeling where more is possible and learning is natural. We can guess, experiment, risk, toss out wild ideas knowing that loving hands will "take and sift them, keep what is worth keeping, and with the breath of kindness, blow the rest away," as Dinah Craik wrote in A Life for a Life.

In 2007, Humanities Montana, an independent, non-profit organization dedicated to bringing the humanities to the people of that state, declared a statewide Year of Civic Dialogue. Citizens had just experienced a frustrating legislative session when leaders did not pass a budget. Civic leaders cited the increase of aggressive and intolerant language across the state, and even cases where people brought guns to public meetings. Perhaps they were on their way home from hunting, but nevertheless, guns in public places do not typically create a feeling of safety! Some leaders recognized they had critical problems with safety, and shared a desire to develop more trust and capacity to work better together in positive and practical ways.

Humanities Montana sponsored a series of conferences called "Can We Talk?" inviting civic, business and non-profit leaders to engage with citizens around the skills and benefits of civic dialogue. They embraced Gracious Space as a way to "put the legs on" civic dialogue and give people tools to show up in less intimidating ways — including leaving the guns at home.

There are many ways to achieve safety. Sharing unusual pieces of information or stories about ourselves can generate discussion about how people feel connected. Using a series of questions that invite participants to share gradually more revealing information will help increase safety.

Certain behaviors and actions will compromise safety and cause an individual or group to regress. The fastest and surest way to erode safety is through retribution. If a person or group shares information that is subsequently used against them, this will crush feelings of safety. The group may muddle along in its work, but the energy will diminish and the container will be sullied. Fear will replace imagination. There must be agreements on how the information shared can be used and re-communicated (or not) by those present.

For several years we worked with an organization that was enthusiastic and progressive in its approach to leadership. They embraced the principles of servant leadership, mentored each other and other employees and continually focused on individual, team and organizational improvement.

One day we asked them to identify limitations to their learning, and how they might overcome these. The question we posed was:

"What patterns or habits within the group are holding you back from being the best leadership team you can be?" Without pause, one person said, "The fact that the CEO is in the room prevents me from being completely honest. I am always weighing how vulnerable I can be because, even though I trust him, I do not want any of my learning edges to come back and be used against me in the future." Another person agreed. "We like the fact that our executives are in this program with us, it makes it more real. But it definitely creates a gap of safety in how much we are willing to open up and learn in public with them watching."

When presented with this information, the CEO was saddened that the members felt that way, but admitted he felt similarly. "I try to be as authentic as I can by being open and a good role model for my group," he said. "But I have limits to how vulnerable I wish to appear in front of my direct reports."

This is normal. Every organization grapples with creating enough safety for people to be authentic and learn in public together, and this can be especially true for leaders, who are expected to provide direction and answers. In Presence, Otto Scharmer writes, "There is no question that one of the greatest needs is how to make it safe enough for people in positions of authority to move [into deep change]."

Another factor that can block real safety is the tension between being superficially safe and being real. When people want to stay at a superficial level of safety, they will not "get real" by voicing vulnerable or provocative opinions or pointing out the moments and irritations that get in their way. The group will find a comfortable equilibrium and hang out there. They will plateau at this nominal level of safety unless they are compelled to engage in experiences that intentionally expand that level.

Probing the discomfort through inquiry is one way to help a group be real with each other. For example: "Where do we, as good people, dispirit each other? How can we inspirit each other?" Or, "Where do we get stuck? What patterns work and which get in our way?" One group dealing with a history of racism asked themselves: "Witnessing the pain in this group, where do we need to bear witness and bring healing?" When done well, these inquiries produce trust. Trust begets safety and safety begets trust. It is as if the group brain rewires itself to entertain more safety and trust through the positive experiences.

Many groups want to assess their safety. How much is there? Do we have enough to do the work we need to do? One way to assess safety is simply to ask how safe people feel. We've used the Five Finger Survey, which asks people to hold up the number of fingers, from 1-5, that demonstrates how safe they feel. We follow that with a discussion about what creates and blocks safety. We also talk one-on-one with people about what they are feeling or hearing from others. By assigning a numerical value, the level of safety can be revisited over time to track movement.

At some point, ready or not, we need to move on to the work. The Four Openings are not intended to be marched through in a strictly linear progression, with one completely achieved and checked off before we proceed to the next. Rather, they are invitations to increase the group's energetic capacity to hold the change work. Sometimes Gracious Space requires an act of faith, leaping into the unknown territory because it matters, and because it needs to be done. As the work gets underway, especially as the stakes get higher, and uncertainties emerge, creating and assessing safety will be an ongoing concern of the leader and group members.

Opening to Relationship

What are relationships and why do they matter? Relationships are the way human beings create and feel a sense of human bonding with others. Relationships are the heart and soul of any group and central to any successful change process. They are the vehicle that carries the work. If the relationships are strong, the group may arrive safely and on time to regions of great possibility. If the relationships are weak, the group or the work may break down in any number of ways. Strengthening relationships is another way to bring in more of the "known," by establishing greater predictability and understanding between people, and freeing members to bring their gifts and contributions. When Opening to Relationships, group members are invited to interact, learn about each other, make decisions together, and jointly define the work that needs to be done.

Through relationships, people start identifying each other's gifts and passions. When passions get tapped, people are motivated to bring more than their skills — they bring their best gifts. Anthropologist Margaret Mead said that 80% of an individual's gifts and strengths remain hidden. "If we are to achieve a richer culture, we must recognize the whole gamut of human potentialities, and so we weave a less arbitrary social fabric, one in which each diverse human gift will find a fitting place."

Writing in the early 1960's, Mead noted that the reason human gifts remain hidden is primarily due to societal norms that frown on "bragging" or tooting our own horns. We undermine our abilities rather than celebrate our accomplishments. We also tend to see ourselves and each other in boxes defined by job titles or resumes. The truth is we are so much more than what we are hired to do, and when we are invited to contribute at that deeper level, so much more becomes possible. When people connect at the level of the gifts they have to offer, they start to own the work. They start to care about other people succeeding and want to make sure that they are doing their part to advance the work of the group.

Strong relationships can be measured by the existence of learning and communication, a feeling of belonging and comfort, and the absence of ridicule, favoritism and exclusion. A quality relationship can give us courage to try new things and discover new meanings. A strong relationship can be a tether or safety net as we venture into the unknown.

Because relationships are invisible, we often neglect them. Relationships *are*; we expect them to be there when needed, and to be permanent and predictable. But relationships are not *things*. Groups working in change efforts must attend to the relationships they are forming. Each relationship is a living system that must be fed and nurtured just like any other living system if we expect it to survive. Try not feeding your cat or your plants for a few weeks and note what happens. Relationships need tending in the same consistent manner.

For too long the work of relationships has been viewed as a soft skill and a distraction to the real work, less important than being efficient and getting results. The pace of life in organizations and communities (even families) is often so frenetic that relationships are overlooked on our long to-do lists. The hard skills of making money, being productive, minimizing costs, managing quality and enforcing the rules become the most important aspects of managing and measuring success.

In 2001, Michael Hammer published <u>Reengineering the Corporation</u>, and made popular the mantra "the soft stuff IS the hard stuff," which quickly became a shared belief among many corporate executives. An engineer by training and a professor at the Massachusetts Institute of Technology, Dr. Hammer showed that while the technology in an organization might work, the people might not. He proved that attention to the people-side of things can make or break an organization. He forever changed how leaders think about employee engagement and commitment, collaboration and communication, development and education, respect and innovation.

Many of today's leaders know that the people-side of the change equation is most important and yet most difficult to get right. People are unpredictable, messy and emotional, yet they are the means by which the work — all of it — gets done, and their effectiveness is paramount to the organization's success.

Daniel Goleman's 1995 book, <u>Emotional Intelligence</u>, drew on brain and behavioral research to demonstrate how "smart" people with a high intelligence quotient (IQ) often flounder in life while others with lower IQ succeed. Goleman explained how this could be possible, and named another measure of success, Emotional Intelligence, or EQ. The factors of self-awareness, self-discipline, empathy, stress tolerance and the ability to be happy, flexible and independent, among others, added up to a different path to success. Goleman showed that emotional intelligence and the ability to relate to others had immediate, positive application to work lives, our personal health and our ability to contribute meaningfully to society.

Unlike IQ, which peaks in our late teens and remains static, EQ can be improved over our lifetime through awareness and practice. "Increasing emotional intelligence makes individuals more efficient, productive, and successful, and organizations can become more productive by hiring emotionally smart people and by offering opportunities to enhance these skills in the workplace," says Nancy Campbell, a certified Emotional Intelligence trainer and consultant who lives on Bainbridge Island, Washington.

The science is finally proving that being relationally smart is critical to success. This indicates that creating Gracious Space is also critical to success, especially in change work, because Gracious Space enables us to explore and deepen relationships.

So if relationships are so critical to our work and our very being, what blocks the development of deep relationships? What causes them to falter or fade? Often relationships fade or fail to thrive simply because we don't *see* them, or don't see them as important or relevant to ourselves. We humans have a habit of looking out at the world from a detached place and considering it separate from ourselves. Psychologist Martin Buber called this the "I-It" relationship, where everything we see outside ourselves appears as an "it," an external object separate from us. From this distance, it is easy to misunderstand, judge, criticize, dismiss and see the other as diminished, dysfunctional and not worth our time. Through this lens, it makes no difference, Buber says, whether the "It" is a table or a person.

The consequences of this arbitrary separation are profound. Not only does such detachment lead to a lack of connection with our fellow humans, it contributes to a vast disconnect between ourselves and the systems we rely on. We live in a time of immense institutional challenges that impact our social, environmental and economic systems. Many foundations of our social fabric are threatened, and this is directly related to our treatment of the "other" as separate. "We have no idea the cost we pay for living this story of separation," says Peter Senge in <u>Presence</u>. "I'm beginning to see that a cornerstone of our work has been simply creating ways to help people connect more deeply with one another, and with their common concerns and sense of purpose."

Fixing these problems is not a technological concern; it is a relational concern. It isn't the "hard" stuff we need to improve; it's the "soft" stuff, but it may be the hardest work we have ever done together. In order to create a future of healthier realities — whether for our family or the world — we must learn to connect and see in a new and truly collective way. Buber calls this the "I-Thou" relationship, where what appears in our awareness is whole and exists in an intimate relationship with us.

We've all had relationships sour, fade or not measure up, or that we've left out of frustration or disappointment. Sometimes the mix of personalities leads to a less-than satisfactory relationship. Many people in frustrating relationships choose neither to grow nor leave, they just hang on in misery. Letting go of relationships that no longer work is part of life, not a mark of failure. All shifts in relationships give us a chance to learn about ourselves. The measure of a good relationship is not how long it lasts but what happens during its existence.

How long should we stay in a relationship that isn't producing the results we want? Sometimes we extend Gracious Space to a person but it seems they are not interested in shared learning and growth. Colleagues have told countless stories of when they invited the 'stranger,' worked hard to include someone who is consistently contrary, negative or not forthcoming, who won't share power or the vision for change, and it doesn't work. They despair that change will ever happen. They ask about kicking the person out. They think about quitting.

A model from David Schnarch's Passionate Marriage: Keeping Love and Intimacy Alive in Committed Relationships, describes how healthy people can make these decisions in a good way. Imagine two concentric circles depicting two cycles in a relationship: a growth cycle on the outside, and a comfort cycle on the inside. In the inside circle of comfort, a person will initially feel good and safe with the other, but over time will start feeling bored, frustrated and detached. The comfort cycle has become too comfortable. At some point the person will choose either to terminate the relationship due to detachment, or take a risk to move to a more expansive level out to the growth circle.

If the person moves to the outer circle of growth, he or she may experience anxiety, caused by change and vulnerability, and confrontation. This is followed either by increased commitment, trust and joy in the relationship as they face the discomfort and break through to a higher level, or termination due to too much anxiety and stress.

This model demonstrates that there are a couple of exit ramps where people will opt out of relationship: too little activity (boredom) or too much activity (stress). The first step is to identify whether we are getting the desired results. If not, we need to consider our choices to improve the relationship. What is the relationship worth? What do we need from the other or the group to commit to the relationship? How likely are we to get it? To give it?

Forming Strong Relationships

Tending to relationships in a direct and immediate way is what philosopher Donald Schön calls reflection in action. Most of the time when we make a mistake with someone, we realize it later and go back and fix it (hopefully). That's reflection on an action that has already occurred. In order to strengthen relationships and for groups to become learning communities, Schön said we need to reduce the time between the incident that causes a problem and when we address it, until we reach a point when we can do it in the moment it occurs. This becomes reflection in action.

"The practitioner allows himself to experience surprise, puzzlement, or confusion in a situation which he finds uncertain or unique," Schön wrote in <u>The Reflective Practitioner</u>. "He reflects on the phenomenon before him, and on the prior understandings which have been implicit in his behaviour. He carries out an experiment which serves to generate both a new understanding of the phenomenon and a change in the situation." Schön called this thinking on your feet.

Reflection in action is just one way to describe a deepening intentionality between people. Groups wishing to engage in Opening to Relationship can try a number of the activities described in Chapter Ten. Any process that encourages sharing information, building trust, creating positive memories, emphasizing commonalities, improving communication, generating shared vision and eliminating structures and processes that keep us separate will serve to deepen relationships.

Eventually the group will recognize it has developed emotional intelligence savvy and a greater capacity for relationship. The Opening to Safety and Opening to Relationship stages of the Change Framework are all about bringing in more of the "known" to develop a strong foundation. When relationships are humming with in-the-moment awareness, reflection and ability to learn together, when they are healthy, vibrant and resilient, the group is ready to open to risk.

Opening to Risk

A poet once said, "A false sense of security is the only kind there is." Hoping for constant security is like hoping the sun will shine all night. It's just not going to happen. We need to prepare ourselves to live in a world without security.

If Opening to Safety and Relationship are primarily about making things known, Opening to Risk and Collective Creativity are about venturing into the unknown. Opening to Risk is a critical moment between the "we trust and like each other" phase of beginning and the "we are ready for action in the unknown" phase of creativity. This is where many groups get stuck — they don't know how to let go, be in uncertainty, open to divergence, invite the 'stranger' and learn from surprise.

Opening to Risk means being receptive to areas of conflict, challenge, paradox, discomfort, turbulence, as well as to possibility and to the breakthroughs that inevitably arise when people work together. Many groups are able to create safety and relationship, but then find that their project plateaus or becomes mediocre because *they don't want to do anything that threatens or damages the hard-earned relationships.* They are unwilling or unable to face the challenges that arise in their work or between each other.

However, Bruce Tuckman showed as early as 1965 in his Stages of Group Development that storming needs to happen and is in fact inevitable, in order for the team to grow, face up to challenges, tackle problems, find solutions, plan work and deliver results. A group that can't or won't move from the forming stage of polite engagement to the storming process of disagreement and pushing boundaries, may be indicating there is not enough safety in place to tolerate the discomfort.

Change work is full of paradox. Running toward the roar asks us to be open to these paradoxes because that is how our capacity will grow. It asks us to let go of some things that have made us safe to this point, in order to learn something new. It asks us to consider the possibility that some of what we are doing could actually be getting in the way of what we most care about. Sometimes the true path lies in the direction that causes fear or discomfort, and sometimes what we thought was the safe route is actually detrimental to our desired outcomes. To move to a more powerful place, groups need to learn from surprise and explore the truth from multiple viewing points. This results in breakthrough thinking, which is not possible when the group stays on a superficial level of safety and agreement.

In Papua New Guinea, the word *moquita* means *that which is known but not spoken.* The communities in Papua New Guinea measure their health by the number of moquitas present: the fewer moquitas, the healthier the community. The same is true for our groups and organizations. In every group, there are things that we can't or won't talk about. When taboo subjects come between people, the relationship shrinks. And the more we have to hide, the less we can do together.

Opening to Risk asks us to name and unpack the moquitas. It asks us to confront the exasperating habits, difficult issues and embedded conflicts that get in the way of being real. We step into the abyss of the unknown, and let go of what we know or can control. Gracious Space provides a safety net so that we can unfold in this way. Often when people take the risk to confront discomfort in Gracious Space, they break through to a more meaningful, trusting and life-giving relationship.

At one organization, two women had worked well together for many years. One day they had an exchange in a leadership meeting that threatened their relationship and embarrassed both of them. One announced an upcoming social event for employees, to which the other inquired, with some negativity in her voice, whether a similar event would also be held at the organization's second location, a temporary site a few miles away. Some employees, including the woman who asked the question, believed the temporary location was unseen and unheard, rarely thought about and often excluded from organizational planning. There was deep resentment about this, which resulted in very tangible tension between the two women in the meeting. After an awkward and defensive response from the first woman, the meeting continued.

Rather than ignore what happened, the two women sought us out to facilitate a conversation in Gracious Space. They named the unspoken feelings, unpacked their reactions, ventured into vulnerable territory, and eventually reached a deeper level of understanding. They resolved the issue, and deepened their friendship and trust in each other in the process.

But they didn't leave it there. They took another risk by bringing their learning experience back to the leadership group that had witnessed the original exchange, and shared their learning in public. They shared a behind-the-scenes look of their meeting, and offered these pearls of wisdom:

- *If you think you're having an emotional reaction, count to ten.*
- *Examine your feelings and motives, in the moment or as soon as possible afterwards.*
- *Ask questions of the other person.*
- *Give others the benefit of your doubt.*
- *If you goof, take time to go back and fix it.*

The impact of their public sharing was enormous and they received a spontaneous standing ovation from the group. But more, the trust level of the entire group palpably rose in that moment. Paradoxically, by going into that which was uncomfortable, the two women helped create more safety and more possibility in the group. Now the whole group trusted a little more that they could be themselves, even make a mistake in front of their peers and supervisors, and still be accepted as a leader. This event marked a turning point for the leadership team that is still talked about years later.

Too often, our cultures are schizophrenic when it comes to taking risks. On one hand, the organization craves innovation, new ideas and new products, but on the other hand, failure is often grounds for being written up or even dismissed. Employees, volunteers and citizens — and our elected officials, board members, CEOs and executive directors — need a buffer when it comes to taking risks and making mistakes. "It is important to provide a level of Gracious Space within the organization so we can share risks and stresses, and raise critical issues without having negative consequences," said Chuck Clarke, former Director of Seattle Public Utilities.

So how do we encourage people to move into entrepreneurial and risky territory? What approaches or supports can we put in place as the group treads into the unknown? Leaders have to be sincere in their promise of no retribution for taking risks. We need to support brainstorming activities, short-term experiments that generate immediate feedback, protect pilot projects from the normal bureaucratic process, generate lots of communication with an emphasis on learning, and suspend disbelief long enough to try something that might work.

We need to enter the risk zone carefully, taking small risks first and testing that safety and relationship are present. In the realm of interpersonal risk, we are not encouraging anyone to suddenly take up every difficult issue in the large group, especially if safety and a strong foundation are lacking. The risk zone is a place where fear can shut down imagination and connection. We each have different levels of tolerance for dealing with risk and uncertainty.

But if someone says something that hints at a deeper issue or a moquita, rather than gloss over it we need to learn to stop and ask, "What did you mean by that?" Joking often masks a real issue that can be risky to address in a serious way. But by naming the unmentionable, and the "elephants in the room" we get issues out on the table, where they have less power over us.

Facilitators and leaders can also make the dissatisfaction with the status quo more tangible and understood. Often groups will not move into difficult change work unless the current situation is disappointing or dissatisfying enough to cause real pain. Spending some time naming what's not working can help the group develop the will to move into the difficult conversation. The key is to use this information as a platform to move to a new place.

We can also pose some compelling questions to dig deeper into the risk: "What do we collectively care about more than ourselves, our habits and our friends? What is the roar in this situation? What would happen if we failed to open to risk? What would happen if we did?" Exploring the work at a deeper level and the consequences of next steps can increase the group's readiness to move into risk. In a group that has been together for a fair amount of time and developed a strong foundation, compelling questions often succeed in helping the group sail through the risk and springboard to creativity.

It is crucial to be very clear about what we want to get out of the risk discussion. What is our goal in addressing the roar or the moquita? Is it to prove we are right and someone is wrong? Or are we really open to discovering and letting go of something that is in our way? How important is it to test and strengthen the relationship by going into the roar together? This is what makes the Gracious Space Change Framework an integral experience. It is not just about solving problems more creatively; it about simultaneously strengthening safety and relationship while we are making better decisions and moving toward the change goal in practical ways. When we allow ourselves to move into this territory, we are on the cusp of truly innovative breakthroughs.

Opening to Collective Creativity

What is collective creativity and why does it matter? In collective creativity, the group works together to create something new. We care about creativity and innovation because, generally speaking, change processes are intended to improve on that which has come before. Even change processes which seek to replicate what has been previously learned must adapt to the current context and be open to novel variations that exist in a particular place. Groups may not even know exactly what they are creating, just that they are willing and able to be in an extended state of uncertainty and thereby remain open to new possibilities. In Collective Creativity we are called to stand together, often in great polarity, and not go to easy answers.

The process of being creative means moving toward what we do not already know. In <u>Presence</u>, Senge writes: "People often believe you need to know how to do something in order to do it. If this were true, there would be little genuine innovation. An alternative view is that the creative process is actually a learning process, and the best we can possibly have at the outset is a hypothesis or tentative idea about what will be required to succeed."

In his DVD, <u>Everyday Creativity</u>, DeWitt Jones, a top professional photographer with the <u>National Geographic</u> and publisher of nine books, describes creativity this way: "Creativity is often thought of as a phenomenon that is larger than life or out of the ordinary, something that belongs only to certain people. Having spent my life in one creative endeavor after another, I can tell you it's not something magical or mystical. Creativity is an attitude. Much of what we call "creative thinking" really results from taking a fresh look — one that is deeper and more determined — at the mundane experiences of everyday life. Creativity is just a moment where we look at the ordinary, but we see the extraordinary."

Researcher Graham Wallas popularized the steps of the creative process in the 1920s in the following progression:

- **Preparation** — characterized by gathering facts and assembling materials. For example, writers get words down on a page or revise earlier work; artists play with the paint or visit a gallery for inspiration. Work groups might review previous efforts or draft a mission statement.

- **Incubation** — characterized by subconscious percolation. We let go of conscious mulling and talking, and our brains go to work while we are doing something else.

- **Illumination** — characterized by great urgency and the need to write it all down before we lose the inspiration. Otherwise known as the "eureka" moment, it often arrives when we least expect it.

- **Verification** — when the idea takes shape into a tangible outcome. Evaluation and reality testing are necessary to determine if the illumination is actually a doable idea that will provide the solution we seek. For every good idea, there are many more that won't ever see the light of day because they don't survive this final stage.

More recently, Dr. Scharmer described in <u>Theory U</u> the process that innovators move through to arrive at ideas. He found that they do not think about past events, but focus on a future they can "presence." In the 'U' process, he writes, "We move down the side of the U, connecting us to the world that is outside of our institutional bubble to the bottom of the U, connecting us to the world that emerges from within, and up the other side of the U, bringing forth the new into the world. At the bottom of the U lies an inner gate that requires us to drop everything that isn't essential. This process of letting-go and letting-come establishes a subtle connection to a deeper source of knowing. The essence of presencing is that these two selves — our current self and our best future self — meet at the bottom of the U and begin to listen and resonate with each other."

The U process is very similar to the Gracious Space Change Framework, in that they both require deep listening, letting go of judgment, seeing the greater perspective, connecting with inner knowing, acting on emerging ideas and embodying the new learning.

When the creative process is undertaken as a group rather than by an individual, the results can be even more surprising. So how does a leader encourage a group to be in an extended space of shared creativity? How we do we encourage a group to explore and push the boundaries together?

The Center has used many different activities to help in the creative process, some of which are described in Chapter Ten and on the Center's website. At one event we hosted for a company, groups of six were given a set of shapes which could be joined together to make squares. Each person was responsible for making one square. No group was finished until all six members made their own squares, and the whole game was not complete until every table had finished. When a table finished, the participants could offer silent support to those still working — but they could not intervene to show the answer. The trick was that there were many ways for the shapes to be combined to make squares but only one way for all six people to end up with squares.

Within 30 minutes, all tables but one had finished. The last table was 80% complete and then got stuck. People were hesitant to undo something that another had contributed. They tinkered with the remaining pieces, but couldn't put them together in an effective way. After 40 minutes, one of the players finally took the squares apart and mixed everything up. The crowd erupted in a cheer, and within five minutes the group put all the squares together.

After the activity, one player realized he was doing the same thing in his new position of Executive Director — holding onto structures that had already been formed while trying to arrange the remaining resources to build something new — and it was not coming together well. The group reflected that organizations tinker with the pieces at the edges all the time. He committed to the group that when he returned he would mix everything up in order to open to the creativity of what could emerge. Within a couple of months, his organization had stepped up to a new bold mission.

The true value proposition for most organizations is to claim what they do better than anyone else. Developing the right products or services that meet today's complex needs requires teams to work creatively. This means that most of our organizations want to work consistently at the level of collective creativity. In order to do so, most leadership gurus say, we have to be willing to fail.

Jim Collins and Jerry Porras, authors of the bestseller Built to Last: Successful Habits of Visionary Companies, discuss the role of creativity and innovation that drives the successful habits of visionary companies. They observe that "some of their best moves were not led by detailed strategic planning, but rather by experimentation, trial and error, opportunism, and — quite literally — accident." It is the willingness to "fail" that makes an innovative process truly innovative and not just incrementally interesting.

An important reminder about creativity comes from David Bohm in Changing Consciousness. Bohm asserts that all thought has a creative function, where the thought eventually becomes something real, which is why we'd best be careful with our thoughts, as they can also create harmful outcomes. "Almost everything we see around us was created from thought, including all the cities, buildings, science, technology and almost everything we call nature. Farmland was produced by thought, by people thinking what they're going to do with the land and then doing it. So without thought we wouldn't have farms, factories, ships, airplanes, governments...So thought can take part in creativity. Thought has created a lot of good things. It is a very powerful instrument, but if we don't notice how it works, it can also do great harm."

For groups, communities and organizations interested in transformational change, it is essential to act collectively while monitoring the impact of the work. Since thought is so powerful, it helps to have multiple viewing points to imagine impacts that are not visible from one particular perspective. The more lenses we have, the more likely we are to think through the whole range of impacts as well as possibilities.

With all this positive momentum, what could possibly block collective creativity? The usual blocks are stress, panic, deadlines and personality clashes, but other blocks to innovation can be more subtle and on the surface even appear to be helpful. These include short cuts, trying to hit a home run every time, and complex products or processes loaded with bells and whistles which real people neither need nor understand. The brainstorm process can become an innovation trap, where the group creates something amazing but which isn't grounded in the organization's values, doesn't really serve the client needs, or is accepted without rigorous validation.

Perhaps the one thing that will kill collective creativity faster than anything else is the need to be right. Rigid rightness, seeing issues as black and white rather than shades of gray, unilateral thinking, intolerance for ambiguity and having made up one's mind — all these versions of thinking where there is only one way to do something — will block openings to new data and will limit an individual's or a group's capacity to be creative and productive.

Summary

The Four Openings provide a developmental blueprint for individuals and groups to increase their energy and capacity for innovation. With the Four Openings, groups can be ready for the change work and be prepared to stay in it once engaged. By paying attention to these openings, the group will begin to make the unknown, known. They will feel safer, develop stronger relationships, be more willing and able to step into risk, and lean into collective creativity.

There are many activities and tools that can help a group into these openings. It is important to reflect on the four elements of Gracious Space — spirit, setting, invite the 'stranger' and learn in public — and consider which of these can most help open up the group. How can the spirit we bring engage people more? Is the setting conducive to building strong relationships and being creative? What 'strangers' or others do we need to invite to truly understand the risk or what's possible? What tools for learning in public could enhance the experience of the group?

Gracious Space doesn't happen overnight or with the flick of a switch. It requires us to make repeated invitations and to be mindful of which aspect of Gracious Space will help this group, at this time, open up to its greater capacity.

The Four Openings
The Four Stages of Change

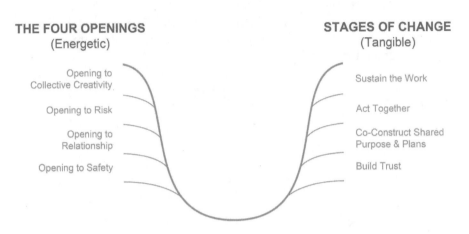

THE FOUR OPENINGS
(Energetic)

Opening to
Collective Creativity

Opening to Risk

Opening to
Relationship

Opening to Safety

STAGES OF CHANGE
(Tangible)

Sustain the Work

Act Together

Co-Construct Shared
Purpose & Plans

Build Trust

<u>Assessing the Openings:</u>

1) How safe does the group feel? Do people understand what safety means to others?

Not safe	2	3	4	Very Safe
1				5

2) How strong are the relationships in the group? Does the group know each others' stories and passions?

Not Strong	2	3	4	Very Strong
1				5

3) Is the group ready to take risks and address hard topics to advance the group's shared purpose?

Not Ready   Very Ready
1   2   3   4   5

4) Is the group able to be collectively creative? Does the group understand the gifts of individuals and how to use them?

Not Able   Very Able
1   2   3   4   5

5) Which opening is the current primary focus of the group?

Safety   Relationship   Risk   Collective Creativity

6) Which elements of Gracious Space are most needed to move to the next opening?

Spirit   Setting   Invite the Stranger   Learn in Public

Chapter Five

The Four Stages of Change

"... it may happen that small differences in the initial conditions produce very great ones in the final phenomena."
— *Henri Poincaré*

The beauty of the Gracious Space Change Framework lies in its integrated nature. In the previous chapter, we showed how groups moving through the Four Openings grow in how they can *be* together. The Four Stages presented here are the tangible tasks of change — what groups *do* together. The stages are: 1) Build Trust; 2) Co-Construct Shared Purpose and Plans; 3) Act Together; and 4) Sustain the Work.

These stages are not unique to the work of Gracious Space. They are part of a model that the Center for Ethical Leadership and partners constructed for collective leadership in the W.K. Kellogg initiative, the Kellogg Leadership for Community Change (KLCC). Indeed, these four stages are common to most change processes. Our experience is that once someone understands the basic steps of change, Gracious Space can take them to a new level of tangible performance. But when leaders lack an understanding of these basics, Gracious Space could create a wonderful learning field that may not necessarily move to action. Taken in Gracious Space, the Four Openings and the Four Stages of Change produce a rich change experience resulting in both internal growth and tangible, positive action.

These stages are not linear. Like the Four Openings, these stages spiral together and influence each other as the group moves through change processes. In each of the following stages, the elements of Gracious Space are needed to keep individuals and the group working together at their best as they address issues concerning their shared purpose.

The Four Openings
The Four Stages of Change

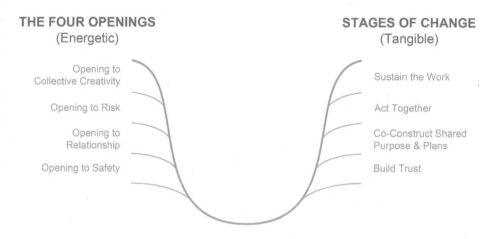

THE FOUR OPENINGS
(Energetic)

STAGES OF CHANGE
(Tangible)

Opening to
Collective Creativity

Sustain the Work

Opening to Risk

Act Together

Opening to
Relationship

Co-Construct Shared
Purpose & Plans

Opening to Safety

Build Trust

Build Trust

Any change process is enriched by bringing together a diversity of experience and perspective. Diversity increases the overall intelligence and capacity of the group, yet the diversity so essential to the work of effective change can also pose its biggest challenge. Building trust is a critical first step in allowing the different talents of those involved to fully come into play. Unfortunately, this step is too often passed over in the premature drive to get to a place of action.

Trust is the binding force of relationships. Building trust is the work of Opening to Safety in general and Opening to Relationships and relationship dynamics in particular. Trust is a quality that, once established, must be cultivated and nurtured through proactive attention, including regularly checking on its status. As new people join the group, trust must be continuously strengthened and renewed.

There has been much written on how to build trust. We find it helpful to think about the component parts involved in creating trust — good character, competence, and consistency. To trust someone, we must believe that he or she has genuine good will and intentions in general and towards us specifically (character), that he has the ability to do the work required (competence), and can be depended upon to follow through on what he says he will do (consistency). If we find ourselves not completely trusting someone, it can help to consider which of these components might be missing. Identifying which component of trust we need from our colleague will help address building trust in as constructive a manner as possible.

The Center has hosted several gatherings known as the Confluence, during which we bring together a very diverse group of 60 individuals to discuss and act on an issue of community importance. At one Confluence, we invited members of groups representing diverse perspectives to explore our trust in public institutions. The entire group articulated what was needed to restore lost trust and how to strengthen it. The group also explored the dimensions of trustworthiness and discussed why it is sometimes appropriate to *not* trust. They concluded that a willingness to extend trust to others stems from our own unique experiences and the environment around ourselves, and that sometimes an authentic response is to not trust.

Increasing trust requires the willingness to make ourselves vulnerable so that others can understand us and have a chance to authentically respond. We cannot do this safely without paying attention to what is going on within a particular context. While we strongly believe that taking risks to build trust is critical to advancing the work, we do not recommend that those working in toxic environments sacrifice themselves by becoming vulnerable to someone who will abuse the trust.

In our work with many groups, we learned that people often assume trust exists because they have worked together on past projects. However, even when we share past experiences, we can still have different understandings of what words mean, what is truly important, what happened in the past, what is happening in the present, and how these happenings are to be interpreted.

People carry hurt and pain from previous encounters with each other or others from outside the community. Until that pain is addressed, it stubbornly informs how much people can open to risk. The negative energy can infect everything we do. As we heard from one wise community change agent, where pain exists, so does choice. There are four things we can do with pain. We can give it back, as in an "eye for an eye." We can pass it on — you hurt me so I kick the dog or yell at someone else. We can hold onto it and silently let it distort us. Or we can transform it, like compost. What we bring to the worm bin is the smelliest, most awful refuse a kitchen can create. But when we let it sit in the right lighting and temperature, it will become "black gold" — soil that nourishes the garden the following spring.

Saroeum Phoung, who shared this approach to dealing with pain, learned from his own experience. He was a Cambodian immigrant who joined a gang as a way to deal with poverty and the lack of options around him. His personal pain included losing a brother in a construction accident and friends to the violence of the streets. When he learned the circle process from a Native American elder and began practicing it with others reclaiming their lives from intense loss and anger, he learned how to transform his pain and rage into love and peace.

In the Gracious Space of a circle process, people share stories and insights about their own role in contributing to the circumstances they find themselves in, and the lessons they have learned. The circle members serve as witnesses — not trying to fix or dismiss — to be with the pain of the person sharing his story. When people first come to circle, they often can stay for only a short time because they are not ready to hear the stories of pain or share their own. As a peacekeeper, Saroeum helped many young people make more positive choices in their lives, first by becoming peaceable members of community, and then by becoming contributing members, able to witness others' stories and pass along the keys of transformation to others.

Building trust in Gracious Space takes great patience, inviting people again and again — regardless of how often they walked away before. It takes honoring the stories and keeping the confidences. Most of all, it takes modeling what it means to dig to the bottom of an experience and bring it up to the light for others to witness. And it means staying in the process for as long as it takes — even if that is years.

Often in our change processes, we are reluctant to bring up the pain of past losses and failures for fear of getting stuck in something we would rather forget. We do not always have the capacity to witness this pain and to move toward the roar, even though we know that this witnessing is a necessary first step in moving through loss and anger to new possibilities. In Gracious Space, it is possible to witness the pain of another without the need to fix it or dismiss it. The point is simply to honor it as an experience that person is having. This is both welcoming the 'stranger' and learning in public.

We can't build deep trust in a group without understanding the assumptions and baggage we each bring into the room, as well as our backgrounds. All this forms a theatre of potentially transformative experiences. Paradoxically, as we strive to build trust, we need trust to name these assumptions, be open to framing past experiences in new ways, and let go of interpretations and stories that keep us stuck in repeating the pain.

The process of welcoming and nurturing the 'stranger,' so key to building trust, involves getting to know each other more deeply. It calls for taking an empathetic approach to culture, personal history, strengths and challenges. Individuals share their values, gifts, resources, capacities and passions. Storytelling in all its forms is a great way for people to learn about each other. Another way of getting to know each other is to map all of the skills of the group. Sometimes people do not see their own skills and it helps when others name for them what they do particularly well. In this stage, the group agrees to work together while honoring differences. Caring people within the group who are willing to witness and support positive movement will help a group become a significant force for good in the world.

Co-Construct Shared Purpose and Plans

One of the attractions of change is that it opens up new possibilities to better serve people. Of course, as the transition is underway, people must be willing to stand in a place of uncertainty and not knowing. Standing in relationships built on trust, the group can open to risk and creativity in finding new ways of addressing their issues.

Before constructing plans, there must be agreement about what matters most in the work at hand. Sometimes a few people are in charge of making this assessment. We have observed that broadening the involvement of those defining shared purpose results in more ownership of the desired goals and of the tasks needed to advance the work, hence the use of the term "co-construct." When people are passionate about a desired outcome, they want to bring their gifts as well as their skills to the undertaking. Having done the work of building trust, people are better able to name what they care about and to feel good about offering their gifts. They trust that others will hear and respect their offers.

In the stage of Co-Constructing Shared Purpose and Plans, there is often tension between the desire to get quickly to action and the desire to take the time needed to incorporate the insights and perspectives of many participants. This tension can also play out as wanting to stay the course once agreement has been reached, while at the same time wanting to adapt to changing circumstances and emerging opportunities. To stand in this tension requires a transparency of shared purpose. When individuals are able to trust that their mates have a clear sense of what they are creating together, each person can assess which individual contributions will advance their overall agenda. Standing in this tension requires that people believe they can influence how shared purpose moves to action.

One KLCC group we worked with moved quickly to organizing a number of projects. We wondered whether the transition was too rapid, we so asked how they decided to stop meeting as a large group and to start working as smaller project teams. The designated leader explained that the whole group was together only long enough for everyone to get a sense of the whole — to see the overall direction of the difference they wanted to make in their community and how they wanted to work together. Once the group had that sense of the whole, the leadership encouraged the formation of small groups. This allowed individuals to act on their passions and to move quickly. Group members were able to tap into their individual creativity early on and generate energy for change. For the youth involved, this was a chance for them to give back to the community after receiving a great deal of support from the organization and they were eager to get going.

We witnessed similar movement in other KLCC groups from many parts of the country, which organized around supporting immigrants in learning their rights, fighting violence by creating new relationships between street youth and the police, and working with the schools to support youth to succeed in school. Each small group incorporated the principles of collective leadership in a different way that honored what participants were good at doing. The organizations they were a part of allowed them to follow their passions and supported them in very significant ways — even shifting organizational direction. Together, they made agreements about how decisions would be made by the group to move agendas forward. With their energy and focus, they involved ever increasing numbers of community members in their projects. Clearly, the groups had opened to safety and relationship, built trust and co-constructed shared purpose and plans by using their collective leadership. This was a strong base for moving to action.

Through this example and others, we learned that when individuals feel connected to the group as a whole and see their work as fitting into a larger pattern and direction, there is an ability to move quickly to relevant action. Individuals feel a greater sense of freedom, flexibility, and power in making their contribution. Participants use their unique and personal gifts in ways that advance the shared purpose, and often in very surprising ways. On the other hand, if the shared purpose is not clear or compelling, then people trip over each other or work unintentionally at cross purposes.

How this play of divergence and convergence is navigated greatly influences whether the next stage of acting together comes together quickly and effectively or slowly and painfully. The good news is that in the practice of Gracious Space, people can share their honest perspectives and determine what they need to stay engaged, and also what they need to give up in order to advance the work of the group.

The stage of Co-Constructing Shared Purpose and Plans can look different for different groups. The following are some patterns we have seen groups exhibit at this stage:

- A group builds a relationship field that is so strong, everyone is nervous about challenging assumptions or naming issues for fear of risking the relationships and the field itself. The more common version is a relationship field that is so weak that people are afraid to challenge assumptions or name issues because they do not feel safe doing so. Either way, the patterns lead to more and more talk accompanied by an often frustrating slowness to action, even gridlock. Until the group has enough relationship capital and the willingness to risk it to move to a new place, it will be hard for the group to set a clear direction and make plans that can inform positive individual action.

- The group identifies the goal that will advance the shared purpose and then allows smaller groups to identify which actions they are passionate about planning and executing. One group we worked wanted to reduce the drop-out rate in a particular school. After conducting interviews with dropouts, they identified that the core issue they could address was improving the climate in the school to support academic achievement and a true sense of belonging. Small groups formed around a myriad of activities ranging from bringing cookies on the first day of school to creating a mentoring program.

- Visionary members of the group identify opportunities and together the group assesses whether these opportunities should be pur-
  sued and what role individuals will take on in advancing the work.

- A leadership team serves on behalf of a larger group or organization to keep the shared purpose in front of the group and uses this
  focus to discern which work is important to pursue. The leadership
  team develops plans on behalf of the group or organization, and
  invites members to perform the tasks needed for implementation.

Regardless of how it unfolds, at this stage people understand
together what is needed to advance the work, and can develop a shared
purpose that graciously accommodates individual passions and gifts.
Using this, they create a roadmap or plan that guides which specific
actions will be taken. The group is finally ready to move into the next
stage of the change process.

Act Together

Acting together is the obvious stage of work getting done.
When needed, there are many leadership tools and practices available
to help groups carry out project management, communication and
effective evaluation. Gracious Space partners with these approaches
by reminding everyone involved that it greatly matters *how* the work is
engaged. Simply stated, the ends do not justify the means; the ends, in
fact, will always reflect the means of getting there.

When those in leadership assume that they should merely
direct people without engaging their many different perspectives, then
acting together becomes an onerous chore at best. Gracious Space
offers the possibility for our individual and collective actions to be life-
giving rather than the viscous stuff of drudgery! Once we have opened
to safety, relationship, risk taking and creativity, we must keep these
openings alive when doing the change work itself. Open and frequent
communication is critical at this stage. Often the group has split into
smaller task groups and needs to stay connected to the larger goal,
especially as new people join or shifts in emphasis occur.

Within the context of Gracious Space, the stage of Acting
Together needs to include paying attention to individual and group patterns, and being willing to interrupt the ones that hinder the work while
supporting those advancing it. Once we are in the thick of the action

(and reaction), the habits and patterns reflecting how we perceive and act in the world come into play. This is often when people of genuine good intention bump into each other, getting angry with perceived prejudices and shortcomings. If the group has not done the Gracious Space core work of building trust and co-constructing purpose, things can start unraveling. If people have not brought in good spirit, cultivated the setting, empathetically invited the 'stranger,' and firmly committed to the transparency of learning in public, then individuals will be prone to retreating to places that feel safer and seem less demanding, or else they will simply exit.

Acting Together requires that time be made for both individual and group reflection. Are people clear about what they expect of themselves and others? Can they be curious and maintain the consciousness of Gracious Space when surprises emerge and events unfold in unanticipated ways? In these moments, we learn a lot about each other and ourselves. It's not always pleasant or easy to look at. Storytelling can be a non-threatening way to explore with each other and make meaning of difficult experiences in ways that respect all voices and perspectives. Humor also helps!

If we have done our Gracious Space practice as individuals and as a group, then when things become difficult it is possible in that moment to entertain forgiveness and compassion for one another. If not, then we must at least be able to find forgiveness and compassion for ourselves as we assess the next step. This is not to say that anger as a response is never justified — only that behaviors that flow out of anger generally carry that energy into whatever happens next. As we noted earlier, anger floods the limbic brain, which encourages flight or fight responses and essentially deprives the neocortex of the oxygen necessary to fuel reason, imagination and creative response. If we are to collectively co-create and inhabit Gracious Space, we must carry it in the moment of action and response, and be willing to reflect and learn as we go, in real time. It is truly a dynamic, open-ended adventure!

It is in this stage of Acting Together that the group raises the questions: Who else cares? Who might be an ally? Who will act in concert and accord with the shared purpose? Traditional strategies tend to focus on convincing potential allies that they should adopt and be part of our plans. The Gracious Space Change Framework includes the possibility of adapting plans to meet the needs of allies, learning in public what commonalities exist and what each might do together that could not be done alone. This approach directs groups to go where there is an opening for change and to find those people who are ready to take a risk to make something better, doing so for the benefit of all concerned.

At the Center, we consider dialogue, storytelling, inquiry and reflection key leadership skills. Unfortunately, these approaches are often considered superfluous once the action is underway. We have found that using these tools throughout the stage of Acting Together is likely to keep the action going in a good way. The tool of reflection, for example, enables the group to hold themselves and individual participants accountable for the commitments they have made to stay engaged and to continue learning. Likewise, using inquiry as the group implements the plan or set of agreements can help the group adapt as needed.

Sustain the Work

One of the challenging aspects of change work is that the work is almost never finished. In organizations or communities committed to ongoing learning and continuous improvement, any completed project or step leads to the identification of another project or step. Often, too, the desired change takes longer and is harder to achieve than was anticipated in the excitement of the beginning. It then becomes important to engage and sustain interest and commitment as each new level of change emerges.

Groups need to clarify what sustainability means in their context. We often think of sustainability as the ability of a project or policy, once begun, to continue over time. Indeed, the success of an initiative may be measured both by its completion and by the length of time the results of the work stay in place. By integrating learning into the long-term results, we add a new dimension to sustainability. The Gracious Space Change Framework gives groups an opportunity to experiment with new behaviors. These new behaviors often lead to new practices that work better than what was done before. As these experiments are replicated over time, they become part of the policies and procedures that support the success of the change work until they, too, need to be revised and updated.

Since the Gracious Space Change Framework is both about the process and the outcome, sustainability means that people engaged in the change work are nourished by the process, as well as that the lessons of working together optimally are sustained. When people do work in life-giving ways and enable those practices to continue, the change work becomes a new way of life. The group not only completes the work in tangible ways, but also creates new means of keeping people engaged. They find ways to welcome new partners. The group adapts the patterns of contribution as it learns more about what works and what does not.

One inspiring example of making the work a way of life comes from an organization in rural south Texas called Llano Grande Research and Development, founded to help youth graduate from high school and attend colleges. As the years passed, the students returned from universities to this small community and started sharing their lessons in creating a better future with the community as a whole. Llano Grande continues to incorporate the voices of returning graduates and to find new opportunities for educational and community development to improve the quality of life in their community.

The cardinal gift of the Gracious Space Change Framework is that it guides change work to emerge out of acceptance, the power of love, and the commitment of participants giving their creative and receptive best. This is at the heart of sustainability. Sustainability emerges where and when people move from doing a job or a task toward taking ownership for advancing the shared purpose. Sustainability thrives as people, in finding strength in community, stay engaged at high levels of learning and are willing to take risks to make something happen that is deemed more important than themselves.

Gracious Space and the Stages of Change

Each core element of Gracious Space comes into play at every stage of the change work. Paying attention to what is happening or not happening in the group with the intention of discerning which of the four elements are strongly in place or need addressing can offer remedies to a group stuck in a given stage.

For example, if trust is lacking, what are the patterns that can be discerned and interrupted? Do individuals need to:

- Do internal work to trust themselves more (spirit)?
- Go the extra mile in fostering a safer, softer environment (setting)?

- Look at ways to expand access to information for those they perceive to be different (invite the 'stranger')?
- Take more risks in sharing what is really going on (learn in public)?

If shared purpose and plans are not coming together, what is needed? Would it help the group to:

- Name more deeply what matters to them and motivates them individually (spirit)?
- Find the right place and time to enable participants to better understand each other's responses to the process (setting)?
- Break open the thinking by considering whether there is some truth in what concerns the opposition (invite the 'stranger')?
- Let go of an agenda that is keeping the group stuck in old ideas (learn in public)?

If the action is stalled or people are not following through, what might be the cause? Has the group made room for individuals to:

- Bring their gifts as opposed to being given tasks that someone else thought important (spirit)?
- Provide more documentation for people to see easily what has been done and what is missing (setting)?
- Let go of trying to make others use a specific approach so that individuals can try their own approach (invite the 'stranger')?
- Take time to reflect and learn together about what is working and what is not (learn in public)?

If people are not attracted to stay engaged in a sustained and full-hearted way, why might that be the case?

- Is the group failing to have fun and to celebrate victories (spirit)?
- Is there a physical place for people to connect often and comfortably (setting)?
- Has the group become an in-crowd that makes it hard for new people to feel welcome (invite the 'stranger')?
- Does the group think it knows how it all works and seeks only to replicate the first success (learn in public)?

It is not difficult for individuals and groups to make this assessment when they take the time to systematically explore where they are strong and which elements of Gracious Space are needed in order to advance their work. It is equally helpful to identify which of the elements are really engaged and to reinforce the patterns that are working well. Remembering to breathe and not take one another or ourselves too seriously can help. Playfulness is part of the domain of Gracious Space.

Summary

The Four Stages of Change provide a methodology that can guide the group through the change process, including helping them identify where they are at a given time in the process and where they need to go next.

Building Trust, groups get to know each other, and individuals share their values, gifts, resources, capacities and passions. The group agrees how to work together while honoring differences. Co-Constructing Purpose and Plans, the group develops a shared purpose that can hold individual passions and gifts. Acting Together, the group builds allies and holds each other accountable for commitments they have made to stay engaged. They implement the plan, adapting as needed. Sustaining the Work means the changes become a way of life. The group creates the means and structure to keep people engaged, welcome new partners, and to adapt the work as needed.

The Four Openings
The Four Stages of Change

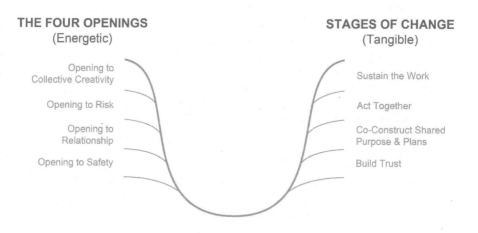

THE FOUR OPENINGS
(Energetic)

Opening to
Collective Creativity

Opening to Risk

Opening to
Relationship

Opening to Safety

STAGES OF CHANGE
(Tangible)

Sustain the Work

Act Together

Co-Construct Shared
Purpose & Plans

Build Trust

Assessing the Tangibles:

1) Which stage of the change process is the group most actively engaged in right now?

Build Trust   Co-Create Shared
Purpose and Plans   Act Together   Sustain the
Work

2) Has the group done the work of the previous stages? If no, what additional work is needed?

3) Types of Questions to ask for the Four Stages

Building Trust	Who cares? Why? What is your story? What matters to you? What helps you be your best?
Co-Constructing Shared Purpose and Plans:	What is possible? What would success look like? Where is it open? What comes next?
Acting Together:	What is working? How can we amplify it? What do you need? What do we need to let go of? Where is it open? What do we do next?
Sustain the Work	Who does our work serve that would want to join us? What do we need to stay connected? How can this integrate with what else is happening? How do we build on success?

4) What elements of Gracious Space are most needed to advance to the next stage?

Spirit   Setting   Invite the Stranger   Learn in Public

Chapter Six

Practice of the Change Agent

"Rather than wishing for change, you first must be prepared to change."

— Catherine Pulsifer

Chapter Four focused on the ways we open ourselves to collective creativity by creating safety, focusing on nurturing relationships and engaging risk to step into the unknown so that we can find new possibilities. Chapter Five offered more concrete steps: building trust, co-constructing purpose and plans, acting together and then sustaining the work. Although presented as separate chapters, these dynamics of energetic openings and action steps are intertwined, playing off each other. How we are affects what we do and what we do affects how we are.

In the center of the Gracious Space Change Framework is a Möbius strip. This symbol represents the inner journey of the individual and the inner life of the group. To review, a Möbius Strip has only one side; it is created by taking a thin length of paper and making one twist, then taping the ends together. If an ant traveled along the strip, it would walk on both sides and return to the starting point without ever crossing an edge. In the model, the two "sides" of the strip represent the distinct but connected and mutually reinforcing sides to the change work. Both individuals and groups must attend to their patterns to identify and transform limits to learning and growth. In this chapter, we make explicit the importance of the role of the change agent in the dynamics of a change process. In the next chapter, we will discuss the importance of how the group works together.

The Inner Work

**PRACTICE
OF THE
CHANGE AGENT**

**WORK OF THE
GROUP**

Why the State of the Change Agent Matters

One of the notable characteristics of Gracious Space — that it embraces change from the inside out — applies to both individual and group transformation. In our experience every effective change effort to make the external world a better place must include work done to be our personal best.

Gracious Space is simple, but not necessarily easy to practice consistently. The practice of the change agent is to explore the territory of the unknown inside herself or himself. This requires as much courage as exploring any other unknown territory, perhaps even more. Each of us has deep patterns that have been encoded in us or developed over the course of time, often a lifetime. The assumptions and beliefs that underlie these patterns exist below the conscious level. Many of the patterns they encourage have roots in deep pain and suffering. Noticing them, working with them, and letting them go involves a willingness to work in unfamiliar, uncomfortable territory. This can bring us face-to-face with the Gracious Space practice of welcoming the 'stranger' within ourselves. Creating safety and building trust within a group becomes more transparent and less complicated when the person leading the effort trusts himself/herself and feels safe in his or her own skin.

We describe this work as a practice because it requires day to-day mindfulness. Each layer of awareness that we develop opens up new richness of experience. As practitioners and leaders we can develop our competencies in offering and exemplifying the four elements of Gracious Space. We must continually come back to how we are showing up and whether or not we are bringing our best selves to the work. And, of course, we need to learn to forgive others and ourselves when we fall back into an old pattern and fall short of our best selves. Forgiveness of others and ourselves is vital in Opening to Safety and Relationship and working through differences as we Co-Construct Plans and Purpose.

One Gracious Space practitioner offered a poignant demonstration of how the day-to-day commitment of the change agent can move change work into deeper effectiveness. Julie was the only Native American employed in a professional position in the local school system. Even though the schools in this town were physically located in the heart of a Reservation, the principals, administrators, teachers, and most of the school board came from the White part of the community.

In the beginning, Julie was angry about the inequities inherent in the status quo. It was hard for her to *be* Gracious Space, especially when she felt she was offering it to those who were not returning it. Yet, she stayed in Gracious Space no matter how others acted, and found this commitment led to better relationships and different types of conversations. Over time, Julie and others worked with the school district to help the school system better serve all of its students. They created a family room that welcomed Native American parents and students, started a mentoring program and performed myriad actions intended to create a more welcoming school climate. It was not easy and not done all at once. In a reflective moment, Julie described her experience of Gracious Space as a journey from anger to hope, made possible by daily practice.

Without practice, Gracious Space can appear to be an abstract concept. Our practitioners across the country continually tell us that in their efforts to bring Gracious Space to their work, they are constantly reminded to live it themselves. "It must be 'in here' first, in order for it to work 'out there,'" Dona from Montana reminded us recently. Fully manifested in behaviors and decisions, Gracious Space becomes a new way of life for individuals, groups and organizations and moves us to our best actions and most innovative responses.

We care about innovation because, generally, change processes are intended to improve on that which has come before, including our own behaviors. The MIT economics professor, C. Otto Scharmer, has done extensive research to uncover how individuals and groups bring innovation to complex issues and processes. In Theory U, Scharmer shares this observation: "Successful leadership depends on the quality of *attention and intention that the leader brings* to any situation. Two leaders in the same circumstances can bring about completely different outcomes, depending on the inner place from which each operates." He observed that the individual leader has a significant impact on the innovation that takes place.

One of our practitioners, Cory, led a church youth group. The youth attended a separate service and felt disengaged from the worship community. Many had stopped attending church altogether. Youth group leaders wanted to meet with the senior pastor and other leaders to explore whether the youth could join the adult service and make it more youth-friendly.

While planning for this meeting, Cory attended the Center's workshop in Creating Gracious Space. She struggled to understand Scharmer's notion that the intention and attention of the change agent has an impact on the change itself. But, she went ahead and prepared the youth to speak directly and respectfully to their elders, and prepared the adults to listen openly to the youth.

A few days before the meeting, Cory was called away to care for her sick mother. After all the work she had done to prepare for the conversation to happen in Gracious Space she would not be able to attend the meeting! She was quite nervous as she left town.

Upon her return, she heard from both the youth and the adults that the meeting was amazing. The adults were relieved and surprised that the youth demonstrated a deep knowledge of the role of worship in community life, as well as an authentic hunger for meaningful experiences. For example, the songs the youth requested were actual hymns — not the hip hop music some adults feared the youth wanted. For their part, the youth felt heard.

Cory was relieved that it went so well, without her even being there. But she wondered, since she had not been there, were her skills as a leader unnecessary? Upon further reflection, she realized the opposite was true. As the change agent, her *attention* to detail and people's fears and desires, along with her *intentions* for an optimistic, reasonable and gracious meeting, were vital. She realized she had played a significant role in the successful outcome.

This recognition, namely that the inner state of the change agent impacts the quality of the change produced, is central to why Gracious Space can play a vital role in change work. Practicing Gracious Space encourages people to address change inside themselves as a critical part of any change effort. Scharmer describes the ways people can address change inside themselves as "presencing the future." Presencing the future begins with opening the mind to let go of judgment, opening the heart to let go of cynicism, and opening the will to let go of doubt. We are delighted that he names these steps because his research clearly moves past the view that change is only a matter of rearranging the external world.

Our response to the external world creates the fire and the desire to find better results that will be of service to those we care about. In our work we have encountered change agents who are motivated for many different reasons. Some are passionate about the earth and are concerned that our continued practices will lead to a planetary environment compromised beyond the capacity to heal and sustain its inhabitants. Others respond to the injustice that they have personally experienced or have seen others subjected to in systems and institutions that organize the flow of services in society. Some are passionate about the work of their organizations and believe that the common good, and the even more brilliant uncommon good, will be served if they are successful in advancing their organization's work.

Given that change agents tend to be motivated by what is happening in the external world, it is natural that they are challenged to take time to do personal work. In the heat and urgency of making a difference, looking inward can feel like an indulgence rather than an essential part of the work. Family systems psychologist Virginia Satir warns, however, that failure to look inward leads to the burn-out that is so common among activists. Unless we grow our own capacity to invite the 'stranger,' learn in public and run toward the roar, we are likely to repeat patterns that contributed to the very issues we wish to address.

Opening Ourselves

Einstein said, "A human being is part of a whole, called by us 'universe', a part limited in time and space. He experiences himself, his thoughts and feelings as something separate from the rest...a kind of optical delusion of his consciousness. This delusion is a kind of prison for us, restricting us to our personal desires and to affection for a few persons nearest to us. Our task must be to free ourselves from this prison by widening our circle of compassion to embrace all living creatures and the whole of nature in its beauty."

This desire to expand our circle of compassion to embrace all living creatures motivates us to do our internal work and to bring good spirit to our change work. Practitioners of Gracious Space believe that we cannot get to a good place in a bad way. History suggests that revolutions born out of anger and violence are far more likely to change who is in power rather than the fundamentals of how power is exercised. At the Center, we believe that evolutions and revolutions born out of a spirit of deep caring, celebration of our interdependence and the desire for mutual responsibility are more likely to catalyze sustainable change that works for all of us.

One of the critical practices of Gracious Space is to consider the way in which each of us contributes to, and is essentially part of, whatever system is in place. It is all too easy to believe that someone else is the problem, and if "they" would change, then it would all work in the way we define as being better. This tendency is particularly powerful when there is a clear injustice in the system and others do indeed need to change. And, the fact remains that the only part we can reliably change is the part that we responsibly own. When we start there, we open up the possibility of changing relationships that can lead to other types of change as well.

In our change work across the country, we have repeatedly seen what happens when individuals move from simply performing tasks in a given project to collectively owning the work as part of an interdependent way of life. When participants became willing to examine how their behaviors were affecting others and the whole, they experienced a deeper level of noticing, took more responsibility, were more capable of forgiveness and stepped into what needed to be done rather than stepping back because it seemed too difficult.

In one agency we worked with, Ginger was hired as a coach to help the group learn strategies such as Gracious Space. She was conscientious and cautious about sharing what was going on for her so as not to "intrude" on the work of the group, even though she was willing to confront other people about how their behaviors were limiting her or the groups' ability to do their jobs. The leadership team did not come together well and the program got off to a rocky start. As time went on and Ginger grew into her role as coach, she began to share what she was learning — including how her own limitations were playing out in the agency and what she needed to do to overcome them. This modeling allowed the others in the group to be more open about what help they needed to be their best.

The youth in this group became more confident and able to give voice to their thoughts and to take the lead on projects. After several years, Ginger was the single remaining member of the original leadership team; yet the practices of collective leadership and Gracious Space were integral to how she and the group operated. When asked what had been the turning point for her, she said it was when she had quit doing a job and had fully owned what it meant to live the principles she was responsible for coaching. This is the heart of the practice of the change agent.

The role of the change agent will shift during the change process as the group moves through the Four Openings and the Four Stages of Change. At the beginning, the change agent often needs to hold the work in an optimistic way and help the group define the work as desirable and doable. The change agent will help structure and guide the movement through the stages and all the work within these stages. As the group deepens their relationships with each other and they start to own their co-constructed dream, the group will take more ownership of its work. At this point, the change agent shifts to become more of a coach — providing feedback and direction as needed, and helping the group reflect as needed.

In his book, The Presence Process, Michael Brown offers a practice to help individuals experience what is happening right in this moment. His basic premise is that each of us is imprinted with a set of beliefs, responses and reactions at a very early age based on what is happening at that time — much of which we hardly understand, but take in nonetheless. As we grow older, these beliefs, responses and reactions play back to us repeatedly, often in unpleasant ways. The way to move beyond those automatic responses is to understand the pattern and to integrate the beliefs and emotions that initiated the chain of reactions at an earlier age into who we are now. It is at that point that we can begin to be present to the moment at hand.

From Brown's perspective, a negative interaction with someone serves as a golden opportunity to see a pattern and become free of that reaction in the future. Brown suggests that any person who triggers a strong reaction in us first be thanked as a teacher. The next step is to let go of whatever that person did and focus on why that action is causing such a reaction. This process requires the courage to slow down, look at our own lives and move out of our comfort zones. The willingness to take complete ownership for our own emotional condition can produce profound results.

When we are Acting Together and Opening to Risk, we encounter many negative triggers, even from people we care about and agree with on most issues. If we can stay in the frame of mind of asking what this moment has to teach us rather than simply reacting in a negative way, our capacity to stay in difficult contexts significantly increases, and consequently so will our ability to guide or lead the change work. In an earlier chapter, we mentioned that freedom is the moment between stimulus and action. We repeat it here because the only way to take advantage of this moment of freedom is the day-to-day practice of stopping the reaction before it takes us over.

Embodying Gracious Space

As we embody Gracious Space in a daily practice, there is no final arrival point or last destination — just a gratifying, deepening level of awareness, one that keeps us noticing patterns and their interactions, and invariably invites a loving and learning response to them. There is no end to inviting the 'stranger' or learning in public. When we use the word "embody," we are inviting people to bring Gracious Space to a level of knowing that comes from the body or at least through it. Here is one person's story about pursuing this level of knowing:

> *"When I was diagnosed with cancer, it was a wake-up call to examine how I was living in my body. I tried different approaches to tune into the wisdom of my body. The Alexander Technique was very helpful. The basic premise of this approach is that right use of the Self (which includes body, mind and spirit) can be developed by paying attention to the relationship of different parts of the body during movement. It requires constant mindfulness to notice the current habit of action, to interrupt patterns and to offer a new direction based on right use.*

Using the technique starts with unlearning old habits of misuse in order to create the base for right use. While a beginner can see dramatic shifts within a few lessons, it can be the work of a lifetime to grow more graceful, centered and effective.

As I gradually let go of my body's tightness and tendency to lean forward, my spirit became more upright and at ease. Western medicine allowed me to cut the cancer out. The Alexander Technique helped keep my spirit and body healthy. The cancer became the doorway into a deeper knowing about the meaning of wholeness."

There are many practices that support mind, body and spirit awareness — Tai Chi, yoga, meditation and some sports. What these have in common is the willingness of the practitioner to pay attention to what is happening in the moment and to keep growing. The practices require both reflection in action and reflection in stillness in order for the practitioner to fully notice what actually works and, in so doing, to let embodied spirit be every bit as dominant as mind.

The performance of these practices is not an endless cycle of blame, judgment and the willful forcing of new behavior. Rather, as an experience existing in time and (gracious) space, the practice is about acting from a place of heart-centeredness and noticing what happens. And part of noticing what happens involves determining when that place and space of heart-centeredness is not particularly present — then simply forgiving and trying again without self-criticism.

Embodying Gracious Space means paying attention to how we show up and the difference that makes — being conscious of preparing ourselves with deep breathing, clarifying intentions, creating good settings and opening our hearts, and noticing when our behavior is not in accord with our intentions. There is no one right way to do this; we must find the practice that connects with our traditions and personal capacities. The more a practitioner embodies and lives Gracious Space, the easier it is for others to open to the Gracious Space within and gain confidence in continuing their own journeys of opening the mind and heart.

A Few Pointers

Archimedes said, "Give me a place on which to stand and I can move the earth." Of course, some places make it easier to move change than others. The place where we stand can be thought of as a leverage point. Some change agents stand in a place of positional leadership and have the authority to make change happen from within the system. Some stand and lead from the edge, and seek to make a positive impact without formal responsibility. From either place a critical factor in leverage is a person's ability to model the behavior they hope others will follow. Groups respond to their leader's behavior, and change agents can model the openness the group needs to try something different and move to a new level. It helps if leaders engage in practices that will strengthen their ability to leverage the desired change.

Good openings set the tone for what follows. Sincerely encouraging all participants to fully bring themselves into the field of relationship can mean the difference between starting well or not. One talented facilitator shared that he always listens to what is discussed before the meeting starts because he has observed that whatever people talk about *before* the meeting will be reflected in the meeting itself. Their thoughts and conversations will course through the group and take the group with it, either in a negative or positive way, on topic or not. Layoffs, promotions, death, divorce, marriage, a public tragedy such as 9/11 or a public celebration of a sporting victory all carry energy that will not be brushed aside. Although groups often reflexively begin a meeting as if nothing important has happened prior to it, addressing what has just come up can either clear the way for a new conversation or enrich the one they planned to have.

Clearing the energy before every meeting will help with this phenomenon. Take a few breaths. Take a moment to check in. Provide a way for people to share what is present for them in that moment, and then ask them to let it go, for now. We will see the relief when people take a moment to vent or name what is going on and consider how they can be more present and able to continue with the real purpose of the meeting. We might ask, "What do you care about right now?" That simple question can shift the energy. We might uncover a nugget of shared concern or a truth that opens a new conversation that takes precedence over the planned agenda.

Do not underestimate the power of simply asking the group to stop for a moment to individually and collectively reflect on whether the process is working for the purpose of allowing all voices to be heard. One of the most powerful decisions we can make as a change agent is to be fully, authentically ourselves — to wonder about what is happening, to own a mistake, to share our gifts and to risk being vulnerable when we need help. The more we do this, the easier it gets, the more comfortable everyone becomes and the more inspiringly Gracious Space is experienced.

All of the above can be achieved by paying attention to the four elements of Gracious Space. As the practice deepens, the change agent will continually find new and more useful ways to bring his or her best spirit, to pay attention to the ways in which time and setting are congruent with the work, to invite the 'stranger' within as well as those people and ideas outside the familiar circle, and to continually learn and let go. Each joyful step leads to a new opportunity to practice and to take oneself lightly. With humor and love, the work becomes enjoyable and nourishing.

A Last Reflection

The following instructions showed up on the Internet one day and describe one perspective on what it means to travel the road of mindfulness and love. It's a bit corny, but it sums up the process of personal growth.

The Installation of Love
Installing Love on the Human Computer:

Customer: Well, after much consideration, I've decided to install Love. Can you guide me through the process?

Tech Support: Yes. I can help you. The first step is to open your Heart. Have you located your Heart?

Customer: Yes, but there are several other programs running now. Is it okay to install Love while they are running? I have Past Hurt, Low Self-Esteem, Grudge and Resentment running right now.

Tech Support: No problem, Love will gradually erase Past Hurt from your current operating system. It may remain in your permanent memory but it will no longer disrupt other programs. Love will eventually override Low Self-Esteem with a module of its own called High Self-Esteem. However, you have to completely turn off Grudge and Resentment. Those programs prevent Love from being properly installed. Can you turn those off?

Customer: I don't know how to turn them off. Can you tell me how?

Tech Support: Go to your start menu and invoke Forgiveness. Do this as many times as necessary until Grudge and Resentment have been completely erased.

Customer: Okay, done! Love has started installing itself. Is that normal?

Tech Support: Yes, but remember that you have only the base program. You need to begin connecting to other Hearts in order to get the upgrades.

Customer: Oops! I have an error message already. It says, "Error - Program not run on external components." What should I do?

Tech Support: Don't worry. It means that the Love program is set up to run on Internal Hearts, but has not yet been run on your Heart. In non-technical terms, it simply means you have to Love yourself before you can Love others. Pull down Self-Acceptance; then click on the following files: Forgive-Self; Realize Your Worth; and Acknowledge Your Limitations.

Customer: Okay, done.

Tech Support: Now, copy them to the "My Heart" directory. The system will overwrite any conflicting files and begin patching faulty programming. Also, you need to delete Verbose Self-Criticism from all directories and empty your Recycle Bin to make sure it is completely gone and never comes back.

Customer: Got it. Hey! My heart is filling up with new files. Smile is playing on my monitor and Peace and Contentment are copying themselves all over My Heart. Is this normal?

Tech Support: Sometimes. For others it takes awhile, but eventually everything gets it at the proper time. So Love is installed and running. One more thing before we hang up. Love is Freeware. Be sure to give it and its various modules to everyone you meet. They will in turn share it with others and return some cool modules back to you.

Customer: Thank you.

Tech Support: You're welcome, anytime.

Anon

Summary

Gracious Space is simple, but not necessarily easy to practice consistently. It is the practice of Gracious Space that brings it to life. For the change agent the practice is to explore within her or himself the territory of the unknown — the unexamined old patterns, stories, habits and reactions. Recognizing the role these patterns play and being open to letting go and relearning new patterns is the courageous role a change agent must step into during the change process. Change agents who hold themselves separate from the change process can actually impede that process, because the inner state of the change agent is integral to the quality of the change produced.

Gracious Space challenges us to recognize that our inner states are a critical part of any change effort, and this recognition enables Gracious Space to play a vital role in change work. As Gracious Space begins to shape our behaviors and decisions, it becomes a new way of life for us as individuals, groups and organizations, moving us to our best actions and most innovative responses.

1) What personal patterns get in the way of being the person I wish to be?

2) In what ways do I wish to shift or support my patterns and habits?

3) Where does my discomfort lie when leading groups?

4) What personal practices do I currently engage in that help me be centered, prepared and able to show up with my best self?

5) Do I need to add any other practices? If so, which ones seem helpful?

6) It takes about 3-4 weeks for a new habit to become part of a system. What checks or milestones can I commit to that will help me be intentional about these changes?

Chapter Seven

The Work of the Group

"Change is inevitable, growth is optional."
— *Bumper sticker seen in Seattle*

The great thing about groups is that they are a terrific vehicle for getting things done. Margaret Mead is quoted as saying, "Never doubt the ability of a small group of people to change the world; indeed, it's the only thing that ever has." The vexing thing about groups is that they can be maddening. People don't always do what we want them to and groups tend to get caught in habits that get in the way.

Every group contains unspoken agreements and disagreements, surprises, conflict, tension, hopes and fears. The inner life of the group contains patterns that can help or get in the way of its effectiveness. Groups need to pay attention to the assumptions they make and what goes unsaid, notice when they are working well together, and be willing and able to move through (not avoid) the difficult spots. Groups need to learn to identify what they must let go of in order to be of better service to the change effort, and allow the process to reshape itself accordingly.

The skill sets involved in this work are many, including holding ambiguity, questioning assumptions, making the implicit explicit, naming the unnamable, illuminating patterns, and identifying breakthroughs. In order to be in this learning space, group members must learn to see themselves as the "we" and not simply the "I" among — and separate from — others. The group becomes conscious of itself as an entity, just as the change agent is conscious of him or herself as a person. The group builds a relational field in which learning and creativity are possible, and out of this process come new narratives, behaviors and actions that contribute toward the desired change.

The Gracious Space Change Framework is a powerful vessel that helps groups and individuals increase their capacity to run toward the roar and collaborate on positive change. This chapter will explore the work of the group in making change happen. We focus particularly on building the relational field, learning to recognize the patterns in groups, and how to amplify patterns that help and modify or remove the ones that do not. By focusing on its inner life, the group can become a vibrant place of learning and creativity for all of its members.

The Inner Work

PRACTICE
OF THE
CHANGE AGENT

WORK OF THE
GROUP

Creating the Relational Field

A *relational field* is a term borrowed from the field of relational psychology and systems thinking, which posits that humans are inherently social and that no personality exists independent of relationships. We know ourselves only through our relationships with others. In South Africa, this belief is called *Ubuntu*, which means, "I am what I am because of who we are." Nelson Mandela used this philosophy of interconnectedness to guide his leadership of South Africa in order to avoid massive violence as power changed hands.

Archbishop Desmond Tutu defined Ubuntu as the essence of being human. "A person with Ubuntu is open and available to others, affirming of others, does not feel threatened that others are able and good, for he or she has a proper self-assurance that comes from knowing that he or she belongs in a greater whole... Ubuntu speaks particularly about the fact that you can't exist as a human being in isolation. It speaks about our interconnectedness. You can't be human all by yourself, and when you have this quality — Ubuntu — you are known for your generosity.

Most of the time, we don't pay much attention to the interconnection between ourselves and others, or to the field within which we are interacting. But this field is a very important part of the interaction because it contains energy, rules, assumptions and potential.

The relational field is an environment that lies latent, ready for us to develop in some way. It can be a place for either negative or positive interactions. When ignored, the relational field will likely be uninspiring, tentative or bland at best, and toxic or harmful at worst. When deliberately fostered with the collective good in mind, this field becomes a supportive environment that cultivates positive and life-affirming relationships. A positive relational field can support us by allowing previously hidden or unknown aspects of ourselves to emerge, and to provide a healing and creative experience. The positive potential for the relational field is always there; but it is up to us to tap into it, nurture it and strengthen it.

There are many approaches to developing a positive relational field. Storytelling, sharing experiences and creating memories, doing projects together, reflection in action — all are ways to tap into and build the relational field. One thing we cannot do, however, is *make* people feel a certain way. All we can do is to provide opportunities for groups to get there themselves, in their own time.

An example of this occurred with one of the community change efforts we worked with. Among participating agencies was an organization known for its capacity to lead circle processes, encouraging people to share in sincere and vulnerable ways. The relationships they formed enabled them to do profound work. Naturally, we wanted this experience for all participants. In preparing for a multi-day retreat with partner agencies, we asked the leader of the first agency to take the whole community to a deep place that would open up the learning for all involved.

She patiently explained that she could not do that. She believed it would be inappropriate to try to take a group somewhere not of their own choosing. However, she said she would be willing to lead a process that would *create the conditions* for people to go as deep as they were ready to go. And as often happens, the presence and depth she brought to the process set up the conditions that made it safe for others to follow into a deeper conversation.

The leader or facilitator's job is to help create the conditions for a deeper experience or intervention, not to produce that experience or intervention itself. A great teacher once said that being a great teacher is about offering your lessons in the best way possible and then being okay with the response — knowing that some people are just not ready to hear them. Set the intention and make the invitation. If the group doesn't follow the first time, they might on second or third offer. Make the invitation more than once, and eventually the group may accept and shift to a deeper place.

Common Group Patterns

Patterns can be helpful or troublesome, but it's safe to say that wherever two or more people gather, group patterns exist. Some patterns are behavioral or emotional responses we repeat with another individual or individuals. For example, in couples: she criticizes, he defends. Or between friends: one talks a lot, the other silently resents or sits back and enjoys. Patterns exist in families — we all play certain roles while growing up, and as adults it is difficult not to fall back into those roles, even if we don't want to. The presence of other family members often pushes us back into those old habits.

Patterns also exist in work groups, communities and organizations. Some are so predictable they have been documented, such as the Forming, Storming, Norming, Performing Stages of Group Development popularized by Bruce Tuckman in 1965. A common name for unspoken patterns that touch a nerve in the group is the "elephant in the room," meaning the truths or assumptions that exist but which group members will not speak about. Group patterns can also take the shape of arguments that get recycled over and over in meetings and conversations. They are the behaviors, assumptions and "ways we do things around here" that we get used to living with, whether they promote or thwart our ability to do our best work. Patterns exist in all forms of human gatherings — in families, departments, communities, states, cultures, and entire nations.

An invitation to Gracious Space can create breathing room to see the patterns at play. Gracious Space can actually serve to inhibit certain group patterns, such as judging, pretending we don't make mistakes, feeling we need to know everything, being certain, and operating all in the head. Gracious Space enables us to let go of these rigid ways of showing up, be less judgmental of ourselves and others, and be more open to possibility.

Many patterns are neutral and their impact depends on how they are played out in the group. For that reason, the list below does not separate "good" patterns from "bad." The work of the group is to identify the patterns that exist, determine which are not helping and need to be let go, and which are useful and need to be amplified. This short list is intended to help practitioners begin to identify which patterns may be present in their own groups.

Common Group Patterns

- Something is created then fails
- Affinity groups form
- We decide everything by consensus
- Apathy is used as a blocking technique
- We carry "baggage" from the past into this group experience
- Small groups that are willing to lead are always the same people
- We may think we're a group, but actually we are many independent thinkers
- We get bogged in detail or indecision
- Old baggage from within the organization shows up
- We forget to align actions with mission
- We have a culture of honesty
- We have a culture of fear and retribution
- It's always been done this way
- Body language (someone falls asleep, texts through meetings, looks at a watch)
- We begin meetings with a ritual
- We don't speak up when we're confused
- We focus on tasks but not the people

- Everyone wants to be an expert
- Meeting norms are not clear: breaks take too long, we start meetings late
- Polarities emerge
- We protect "the elephant" in the room
- Someone tries to fix others
- We stay at the surface instead of going deep
- We avoid conflict
- Someone goes on and on and we want them to stop but don't say anything
- Two people get into an argument and go back and forth
- We spiral down to the worst case scenario, usually lack of money
- Non participation by members
- We have a history of not trusting each other
- We don't know how to interpret or interrupt cultural patterns
- There are dominant talkers and quiet people
- We think we aren't smart enough, or need someone with more clout, knowledge, contacts, money, etc. to make decisions
- People are polite and don't say what they think

So if we know what the common group patterns are, why can't we just shoo the unhelpful ones away? The nature of a group pattern is that it will persist even if we see it, name it, and wish it weren't so. The status quo of systems — frequently called inertia — exerts a powerful force even if we want to change. Patterns take attention and intention to undo.

For example, in one health care organization, nurses complained about not being able to provide the highest level of customer service because of the bullying personality of one of the doctors. "He bursts into the room, interrupts, yells at us in front of the patients, and expects us to do what he says with no regard to the impact he has on everyone around him," said one nurse. "People are afraid of him. We don't want to work with him, and our patients think we're crazy to put up with it or they want to run out of the room after one of his explosions. It's unacceptable."

Yet the staff had gotten used to it. The behavior of this doctor and the nurses' reactions to him is a common pattern that often evolves in systems where "experts" are perceived to have (or are handed) more power, and therefore behavioral latitude, than the rest of us. Often called "protecting the maverick," this pattern commonly tolerates abusive behavior from subject matter experts and others high up on the food chain. In this example, nurses swallowed their feelings and found ways to work around the doctor. This pattern was extremely destructive but no one had the courage to approach the doctor in Gracious Space and start a conversation about changing the pattern.

Patterns can also be positive. A former Seattle police chief shared a story about the pattern of that city at night. While interviewing for the post of chief, he stayed at a downtown hotel. Late at night before he had decided whether to accept the position, he stood looking out the window. The streets below were empty of traffic, but a pedestrian approached the intersection. The soon-to-be chief expected the pedestrian to jaywalk since no cars were around, but the person didn't. Instead, the walker waited for the light to change, then crossed. At that moment, the man in the window decided he wanted the job of chief of police. He wanted to be the police chief of a city where people followed the rules even when they thought no one was looking. The behavior he observed was indicative of a pattern in Seattle for a peaceful, rule-abiding community. The chief and his department went on to create an innovative Community Policing model that built on the good will of citizens and police to create a safe community.

Identifying Patterns

Having knowledge of common group patterns and where groups tend to get stuck is valuable for anyone wishing to deepen their ability to work in the Gracious Space Change Framework. Practitioners can observe, listen, inquire, and attempt to name the pattern that is happening. Some people are tuned in and can easily name a pattern, even if it's unspoken. They can say, "There is hurt/fear /joy/anger/or some other energy or emotion in the room." This is an amazing gift.

But what happens if we are not that intuitive, or don't trust the intuition we are experiencing? What happens if we suspect someone is projecting something *they* feel onto the group and calling it a pattern? And most frustrating of all, what if we just can't *see* it?

The good news is that identifying and naming patterns are skills we can develop. When we develop the skill of seeing our own patterns, it's called self-awareness. In the book EQ Edge, authors Stein and Book define self-awareness, an aspect of Emotional Intelligence, this way: "The ability to recognize your feelings, to differentiate between them, to know why you are feeling these feelings and to recognize the impact your feelings have on others around you."

One way to improve our self-awareness is to tune in to what we are feeling in the moment. Every so often, check in and ask a question like one of the following:

- What am I feeling?
- Am I engaged, confused, bored, sleepy, angry?
- When do I feel at my worst? What is happening then?
- When do I feel at my best? What is happening then?
- Do the same kinds of things keep happening to me?
- Do I keep attracting the same kinds of people, jobs, relationships, etc?

When we recognize a feeling and realize that we have this feeling often, this usually is indicative of a personal pattern. Sometimes our feelings (and our emotional well-being) are at the mercy of a relationship, that is, someone else's actions determine our responses. In this instance the pattern is one of allowing someone else's story to become our own. When this happens we need to stop, check in, note our feelings and where they are coming from, or note the story we are telling ourselves about what is happening, and decide whether this is true or helpful to us. If not, it is best to jolt ourselves out of dwelling on these feelings and move on to something more constructive.

The chances are good that if we feel a certain way in a group, someone else does too. We can check for a pattern simply by asking about it, for example: "Is anyone else confused about what we are doing right now?" The questions above can also work for groups trying to indentify patterns.

Sometimes it is difficult to see what is going on around us because we are in the thick of it. It's like the saying, "A fish doesn't know it's in water until it's taken out." Changing our perspectives by visiting another organization or community group, reading material from different industries or talking with people outside our fields are good ways to invite the 'stranger' and new views on our own patterns. It is also valuable for an outsider to offer observations to the group. An external change agent or consultant, or a trusted and credible ally, are good ways to get feedback on what may be happening in the group.

Getting feedback from either within the group or from outside will move the group to a greater awareness of itself as an organism with its own unique habits and patterns. The inquiry or observation is actually an intervention into group process. It's like taking the pulse or temperature. How are we feeling with this? What do we think about how we are feeling?

If enough members feel the same way, and if this particular situation happens often with this group, we likely have named a group pattern. It can be very helpful at this point to acknowledge this as a pattern, because then the group can turn its attention to whether this is a helpful or unhelpful pattern, and from there make choices regarding what to do about it. Oftentimes there will be disagreement about what is going on. Some may agree with the perspective offered, but others will offer up very different perspectives, a dichotomy which indicates there is widespread confusion that no one was mentioning. This in itself is a common group pattern!

This situation occurred at one of the early Gracious Space trainings. On the second morning, the three facilitators asked participants to share their thoughts and questions about the previous day. The conversation became a wide-ranging series of comments, and we soon veered off the advertised agenda. This went on for about 30 minutes, until someone asked: "What are we doing right now? I'm confused."

From the facilitators' points of view, we had tacitly agreed (through eye contact) that we would allow the conversation to emerge, because we felt it was useful to get people's questions and observations out in the open. But when we checked in with the group, they had nearly ten different perspectives on what was happening in that moment! We were rather embarrassed and confused ourselves, so we took a break, which is a good way to interrupt a pattern.

During our facilitator huddle, we realized the group had just experienced a number of common group patterns, and since exploring group patterns was next on the agenda, we decided to use the experience as a laboratory into the nature of group patterns. When we reconvened, we shared our thoughts concerning what had transpired and took responsibility for not being clearer. Then we asked people to re-visit the morning conversation and use it to surface the patterns they thought we experienced as a group. People were open-mouthed with amazement that they had fallen into some of the same patterns that drove them crazy in their own groups. They named several on the list above, including letting dominant talkers have the floor, not wanting to ask a "dumb" question, and simply enjoying the conversation and not worrying about where we were headed.

The debrief was rich with learning, and participants were able to apply their experience to other patterns they had come across in the past. The facilitators, too, learned a valuable lesson: if we venture off agenda, make sure everyone is with us. And, we learned that a silent agreement among three people in the group — even if we were the facilitators — is pretty much like not having agreement at all! Anyone else ever experience that pattern?

Interrupting the Pattern and Getting Unstuck

Once the practitioner or group recognizes an unhelpful pattern, we have the opportunity to interrupt it. It's all about rewiring the circuits in our collective brain. We become wired to act and react in the same predictable ways. For individuals, there are techniques to stop ourselves from acting out our programming even when we're right in the midst of it. We can shout, snap a rubber band on the wrist, or stand up. The startling effect interrupts our regular brain patterns.

We can do similar things that startle in groups. Participants can stand and stretch. They can change seats, which is especially provocative in a bargaining or negotiating situation — we ask the representatives to sit in the other's seat and experience the other's point of view. Taking a break, checking in with a few members, or asking them to talk in small groups are all ways to interrupt a pattern.

We have gathered many suggestions for how groups can shift out of unhelpful patterns once they are identified. All of these methods involve an aspect of reflection and dialogue, so there first must be willingness and capacity in the group to explore the areas of stuckness together. Working with the Four Openings of Safety, Relationship, Risk and Collective Creativity directly impacts a group's ability to interrupt the action and reflect in the moment. Having experience with and a commitment to inviting the 'stranger' and learning in public is vital. Using shared language, whether from the Gracious Space Change Framework or another method, also makes it easier. Maybe one of these activities can help a group move out of a stuck place right now:

Ways to Interrupt a Pattern

- Take a break
- Ask a question
- Name the pattern and start a conversation
- Name the "elephant" or unspoken thing
- Let go of the agenda and be present with where the group is right now
- Make sure decision makers are on board for the change; otherwise you'll have to go back and re-engage them
- Change formats, meeting rooms, leadership roles or procedures
- Draw or act out the group's experience
- Hold a ritual to cleanse or heal
- Stop the interaction and invite people to listen for something new in silence

- Make an observation
- Form small groups to discuss what is happening and report back to the whole
- When people get quiet, ask, "Are we stuck, or just still?"
- Stop moving toward a solution
- Ask clarifying questions and help people feel heard
- Allow venting in a structured way
- Make it ok to be in chaos
- Refer to procedure to make a decision
- Experiment with new ways to do things
- Make public commitments to new behaviors
- Check out stories people are creating or assumptions they are making

Some patterns are so deeply ingrained that it can take months or years to see them. These are often inherited patterns — ones that have been woven into a system for so long we simply don't realize they are there.

We worked with a family-owned business experiencing mistrust in the business and family relationships. During a retreat facilitated in Gracious Space, the group built safety and trust, then worked its way through several unhelpful patterns. First they addressed interpersonal grievances that kept arising between pairs of people. For example, mother and daughter, who were also the board chair and leasing manager, or the cousin and grandmother, who were also the groundskeeper and the chief land steward. Then the group moved to uncover some of their "moquitas" — group patterns that had remained unspoken but which people had learned to live around with resentment or confusion. On the third morning, the grandmother had an insight that moved the group into the powerful, hidden territory of inherited patterns.

One of the resentments to surface earlier was the appearance that the eldest male child was given all the breaks. He used the facilities for personal clients while others were told they could not. He made a bad, personal, financial investment and got bailed out by the business. On the other hand, he was expected to manage the family business profitably in perpetuity, but no one knew if this was even his passion; it had always been done that way, so they expected it to continue.

Grandmother said, "Don't you see what's happening? This is the "golden boy" phenomenon. We inherited this pattern from our ancestors: that the eldest male will run the business, whether he wants to or not, and any brothers, sisters or cousins simply cannot have a place in it." The group fell silent as the truth hit them. "We have the choice, right here, right now, to end this pattern. We do not have to accept the legacy of the 'golden boy.'"

The eldest male admitted how alone and afraid he felt due to the unspoken burden he had assumed since he was a boy — and he had never even realized it. The women in the room exclaimed how they had never been allowed to truly own parts of the business they loved. The group agreed with heartfelt angst and hope to discard the old pattern. They held a ritual to cleanse the family business of the old pattern and the hurtful relationships it had caused, so they would never be blindly governed by it again.

Fortunately the group possessed the right ingredients to shift the pattern: they had the courageous conversation and the "aha" moment together; they allowed structured venting and were willing to be present with what was emerging; they had the decision makers in the room to agree to a new way; they generated several behavioral and structural changes to create new, more helpful patterns; and they agreed to remind each other in friendly ways when they strayed from the new ways of doing business and living together as a family.

Reinforcing Positive Patterns

Pattern work is not always about identifying and ridding ourselves of negative patterns; it's also about claiming and reinforcing positive patterns. Reinforcing positive patterns doesn't happen automatically. We need to pay attention to make sure that which is helpful doesn't fade away from lack of nurturing, especially when these patterns are unspoken. Sometimes just naming the good habits is enough; sometimes we need to notice, celebrate and formalize them. We sometimes call this practice "catching people doing something right."

The family in the example above also illuminated patterns they wanted to hold onto, such as gathering often as a family to deepen their personal relationships. They created new ways of communicating and working together, such as the mother agreeing to call her daughter for mother-daughter chats, not just for business. They formalized some of their decisions in new policies and structures for the business. They held another retreat six months and then a year later to reflect on how the new family and business patterns were working and to give each other feedback on how to tighten and sustain the ones that were working well.

Many of the activities for interrupting a pattern noted earlier also serve to amplify the positive ones. Here are some other ways to reinforce positive patterns.

Reinforcing Positive Patterns

- Name what you care about
- Make public agreements to continue doing what's working
- Start new behaviors or systems that align with positive patterns
- Post visible reminders
- Update the groups' "story" or mission
- Make it okay to make mistakes
- Formalize or make intentional the good habits and outcomes
- Make statements of appreciation
- Take time to reflect on what's working

- Write something and then read it
- Celebrate successes and accomplishments
- Research and highlight best practices
- Provide resources to support best practices
- Spread good habits and practices to other parts of the organization or community
- Provide rewards and incentives
- Agree on ways to gently remind each other
- Revisit the conversation frequently and adapt as needed

Making New Patterns Stick

Once we illuminate a pattern and agree to change it, it may seem like our work is done. Relief! Not quite — we need to make the change stick. We need to make the new story real and sustained. After a week or two of concerted effort, people will get busy and forget. Remembering the new habit or pattern will feel like too much work. The weighty inertia of the status quo will threaten to pull people back into the old pattern. It takes intention and attention to make the change stick.

Some Native American groups say it takes 30 days — one lunar cycle — to make a new habit stick. In his book Psycho Cybernetics, Dr. Maxwell Maltz notes that it takes 21 days for a new habit to form. Originally a plastic surgeon, Dr. Maltz noticed it took three weeks for amputees to cease feeling phantom sensations. He noticed it took the same amount of time for the human mind to adapt to any significant life change, whether the loss of a limb or loved one, a change of employment or residence, or a positive event such as entering a new relationship or new behaviors.

Dr. Maltz speculated that brain circuits will produce new neuropathways only if they are bombarded with the new information for 21 days in a row. This means that our brains do not accept new data for a change of habit unless it is repeated each day for three weeks. Dr. Maltz's research formed the genesis of the "21-Day Habit Theory," which has become an accepted component of self-help programs.

So we need to give the new pattern three or four weeks of repeated, daily effort. It helps to have visual cues and reminders, for example, posting decisions and agreements on the wall of an office, or making copies to give to participants. It also helps to have an agreement to gently remind each other when we fall back. We also need to forgive and support each other as we come to terms with new behaviors.

There is a role for humor here. Gracious Space is often perceived as a space of earnest inquiry and exchange — and it is — but it can also be a place of laughter. The fact is, most of us learn more when we are loosened up and laughing. We can choose to deal with our idiosyncrasies and goof-ups in humorous, nonjudgmental ways rather than with shouting or stony silence. Sometimes we call this "falling-on-your-face space."

An exercise we often introduce to groups moving into Gracious Space is called "I failed!" We ask people to stand and demonstrate the body language of failure; people slump their shoulders, look down at the floor or wring their hands. Then we ask them to show us the body language of victory. Hands go up in the air — hurrah! Next we tell them we are going to create new cellular memory as it relates to failure. When you goof, throw your hands in the air like a victory and shout, "I failed!" We do the victorious action and repeat together three times. "I failed, I failed, I failed!" Everyone shouts together with arms in the air and big smiles on their faces. Creating new responses to failure is exactly what is needed to rewire circuitry and remain in Gracious Space. After all, is it really failure if we learn something from it?

Several groups we work with have adopted this simple but fun-loving behavior. One young office assistant was asked to complete a complicated printing project on deadline. When her boss asked her for an update, the young woman stood up, threw her hands into the air and said, "I failed!" The boss said, "After that, how could I possibly reprimand her?" Laughing, they worked together to fix the problem. Similarly, the Chief Financial Officer of a large public agency hosted a Gracious Space training for 100 members of his staff. When he visited at the lunch break to introduce a special video, the equipment failed. Rather than get flustered, he turned to the attendees and put his hands in the air without saying a word. Instantly the group broke into laughter, relaxed and waited with a different spirit for the problem to be resolved.

Each interaction is an opportunity to solidify positive new behaviors. Moment by moment, experience by experience, we change the story and we change the culture. Quite soon, perhaps as soon as three weeks later, we may look up and realize that the stubborn, old pattern no longer exists and we are in a new and healthier place.

One of our practitioners runs a leadership camp for middle school boys who are underprivileged and who do not have a lot of experience with conventional success. During one session, Mike led an activity with the boys called the trust fall. In a trust fall, someone stands on a platform such as a table, crosses his arms over his chest and falls straight back. The people on the ground stand in two lines facing each other, with their arms extended, and are entrusted to catch the falling person.

Mike is about 6 feet, 5 inches tall and built like a football player. After prepping the boys on how the exercise worked, he climbed onto the table, crossed his arms over his chest and fell back...and back... and landed on the ground. The boys failed to catch him. Now if it were us, we might say, "You know, I'm not so sure I'll keep this exercise in my repertoire." Or maybe, "What can we expect — these boys are not used to taking responsibility for their actions." Certainly, we wouldn't do it again. But Mike got up and climbed back on the platform, and fell back again. This time the group caught him.

The stunning lesson here isn't that Mike had courage, although he surely did. The beauty is that he gave those boys an opportunity to change their story — which was that they were untrustworthy ne'er-do-wells from whom society should expect little. We can only imagine where they might end up if they played that story out. But that day with Mike, their story changed. They became boys who worked together to catch a large man falling through the air. They became responsible for their actions and for the welfare of someone else. And those boys will almost certainly be better men because of it.

Summary

Groups working in change form a relational field that can be nurturing, destructive or simply lackluster. Groups need to intentionally create a positive field in which they can attend to both task and process. The Gracious Space Change Framework illuminates the inner work of the group, including patterns of stuckness and highlights opportunities to learn and work better together.

Assess the spirit of the group (relational field):

1) When the group comes together, what is the predominant energy or spirit that is present?

2) How can we intentionally create a more positive field?

Assess Patterns:

3) What unhelpful patterns exist in this group? How can we end or shift these?

4) What positive paterns exist in this group? How can we claim and reinforce these?

5) What new patterns do we want to develop?

6) Which elements of Gracious Space could help the group right now to deepen its experience and be more aware of itself and its patterns?

Spirit   Setting   Invite the Stranger   Learn in Public

Part Two

The Gracious Space
Field Guide

"Miracles come in moments. Be ready and willing."
— *Wayne Dyer*

The Gracious Space Change Framework invites change agents to be flexible in their approaches when applying Gracious Space to their specific contexts. There is not one straightforward scripted method, nor does the introduction of Gracious Space proceed the same way for each group. Rather, the Gracious Space Change Framework provides a palette of choices and entry points from which the change agent can draw to assess where the group is, find the pockets of openness, and determine the best approaches for the group at that time. Working with diverse people in lively situations of change necessitates a dynamic and receptive approach. The possibilities are wide open, with many ways to take the work.

We acknowledge this can be daunting. Many of us would prefer a silver bullet or failsafe five-step program that would deliver consistent results regardless of circumstance. Our research indicates that some practitioners encounter obstacles or trepidation when it comes to applying Gracious Space. Even though people can *be* Gracious Space in their intentions and personal style, they hesitate when it comes to *doing* Gracious Space, especially in entrenched work or community settings. They either do not have a sufficient tool box of activities and processes to support their work, or they lack the confidence or experience to predict how the tools and processes will play out over time.

This Field Guide is intended to address these issues of readiness and application. The Center for Ethical Leadership's goal is to deepen and spread the understanding and application of Gracious Space in organizations and communities across the country and throughout the world. This section serves as the handbook for Gracious Space Practitioners, providing tools and practical approaches for getting started and applying Gracious Space over time.

The section contains three chapters: Chapter Eight) Assessing and Developing Readiness; Chapter Nine) Case Studies that demonstrate Gracious Space in different contexts; and Chapter Ten) Tools and Activities to Establish Gracious Space. These chapters should help internal change agents (employees, executives, managers, program directors, etc.) and external change agents (consultants, facilitators, mediators, etc.) weave a Gracious Space strategy that honors where a group is and where the group wants to go.

For immediate reference to tools and activities, visit the Gracious Space Practitioner's page on the Center's website at www.ethicalleadership.org.

Chapter Eight

Assessing and Developing Readiness

> *"Whatever you can do or dream you can, begin it. Boldness has genius, power and magic in it."*
> — *Johann Wolfgang Von Goethe*

This chapter will help change agents be bold and courageous in their use of the Gracious Space Change Framework, right now. We believe that genius, power and magic will result. We start by assessing readiness, which includes identifying a group's natural strengths, identifying the pockets of openness, and evaluating the group's culture — whether open, neutral or hard — which affects the group's ability to use Gracious Space successfully. Every group has strengths to work with and build on. Every group has pockets of openness where Gracious Space can take hold. And, every group has a set of dynamics that characterizes how its members interact and will indicate how open or closed it will be to using the Gracious Space Change Framework.

The only mistake a leader can truly make with Gracious Space is not using it. We've had practitioners describe how they tip-toed around the term Gracious Space for years, calling it something else and offering up tiny tidbits and activities, afraid their groups would rebel. When they boldly claimed Gracious Space, the groups, in most cases, responded enthusiastically at the clarity and enlightened possibility of Gracious Space.

Assess Strengths of the Group

When we look for the strengths of a group, community or organization, we are looking for traits such as trust, honesty, collaboration, learning, welcoming different ideas, and dealing constructively with conflict. Below are some strengths to consider in assessing group readiness for Gracious Space. There are many other strengths we could consider; the point is to find what the group does well and start there. With a group in mind, assign a rating to each strength and then reflect on where the natural strengths lie within the group.

Group Strength Assessment	1 (low)	2 (mid)	3 (high)
1. Trust and a feeling of safety among members			
2. Being honest with each other			
3. Ability to give and receive feedback effectively			
4. Collaboration			
5. Ability to inquire into judgments, assumptions and patterns			
6. Open to, and inviting of, differences			
7. Skills for having difficult conversations			
8. Skills for resolving conflict with respect			
9. An environment that supports reasonable risk-taking			
10. Ability to admit mistakes			
11. Willingness to learn together and from each other			
12. Willingness to ask others for help			
13. Genuine compassion and regard for each other			
14. Willingness to commit resources for development			
15. Sharing power			

The high score areas are natural starting points for building on Gracious Space. The leader and the group can explore these areas more fully, inquiring into what works well, why it works, and how the group could do more of the same. If many scores are low, the group will need to attend to these areas. For help building a foundation of readiness, refer back to the sections on Opening to Safety, Opening to Relationship, Opening to Risk and Building Trust in Chapters Four and Five. Chapter Seven on The Work of the Group has information about how to identify group patterns, enhance those that are helpful and discontinue those that are damaging.

One leadership team we worked with initially scored fairly low on most of these items, with the exception of a willingness to commit the resources for development. The Executive Director was steadfast in his belief that leadership development for his directors, managers and supervisors would create a premier workplace with top-notch customer service.

His commitment stood the test of time through four budget cycles, 50% staff turnover and a lengthy economic downturn. While similar organizations were cancelling their leadership development initiatives, this group protected their investment, even though they had to make some cuts. Over the course of three years, the group experienced significant, measureable improvements in all of the strength areas. They "hired up," to bring new people on who were aligned with the leadership goals. They integrated Gracious Space into their customer service program, board meetings, staff meetings, executive retreats, budget planning process, supervisory training programs, mentoring program and performance appraisal systems.

Find Pockets of Openness

The next step is to identify pockets of openness. By this we mean finding the people, events and goals that align with the principles and practices of the Gracious Space Change Framework. Identifying these openings will help practitioners develop a strategy and allies for introducing Gracious Space, including specific activities and experiences that match the group's needs and leverage its strengths. When Gracious Space fails to take hold, it is usually because the change agent failed to find an opening, and instead engaged in a frustrating attempt to knock down doors and unblock ears. Here are some angles to consider when looking for ways in. Remember, it only takes a small opening to create the space for profound transformation.

❖   **Find a champion.** Practitioners of Gracious Space are wise to partner with others who are heading in the same direction. Who is open to the concepts and practices of Gracious Space? Who might be a champion for more collaboration and honest communication? Who is ready for a more collective leadership strategy? Find someone who understands the need for a better way to communicate, collaborate and lead change. Try to find someone with leadership authority and, even better, a budget.

One of our Montana colleagues strongly believed that Gracious Space would help local city council members work better with contentious issues. She interviewed a few council members, and found one who was willing to read the first Gracious Space book and have a conversation about it. He could see the possibilities and was willing to continue the conversation with her, until he felt ready to be the internal champion with his peers. Then, with her help, he suggested a few activities for the council's next retreat to open the space for new ways to work together.

In another organization, the Chief Financial Officer was a big fan of Gracious Space. The fact that he was sponsoring workshops for his staff about an approach that calls for trust, interdepartmental collaboration and communication surprised many of his co-workers, who expected him to be just another "typical numbers guy" focused on the bottom line. His ability to champion Gracious Space provided an opening for many employees who were initially skeptical.

In the city of Burien, Washington, the mayor and deputy mayor attended a Gracious Space training and returned to city hall determined to change how the council related to the citizenship. Over several months, they introduced one small shift or activity at each council meeting. For example, the mayor physically moved her position from the center of the table to a side seat and gave other council members an opportunity to lead the dialogue. They introduced a public discussion period at every other meeting. They began meetings by asking what the council loved about their city. They brought in a Gracious Space facilitator to the council retreat to deepen the experience.

"We learned to open ourselves to the people we represent and share what is positive," said Rose Clark, Deputy Mayor. "We needed to turn the pyramid upside down so the government process was not driven by the hierarchy, but driven by the people. Our city will definitely benefit from Gracious Space."

Sometimes an external facilitator can be the champion. The facilitator can hold the possibility of a better way until the group owns it themselves. For example, one small group was struggling with very contentious issues and didn't believe they could deal with them fairly on their own. The presence of a facilitator gave them the safety and permission to do so, and the Gracious Space Change Framework provided a guide to address long-standing, difficult issues. The fact they were paying for a facilitator provided incentive to make real progress while she was present. At the closing, they said, "You trusted the process when we couldn't. You knew a shift was possible, and you held it as a possibility until we could believe in it ourselves. You held the container of safety and fairness, and we couldn't have done this without you."

❖   **Find or create a positive peer group.** A peer group can directly impact whether a change process is accepted or rejected. A positive peer group is formed by natural connectors who will adopt and help spread the intent and practices of the Gracious Space Change Framework. Positive peer culture is a concept that leverages peer pressure to steer the group in a positive direction. Peer pressure is typically thought of as a negative stimulus, such as when kids do something they shouldn't because a friend dared them. Positive peer culture draws on the same tendency to influence, and be influenced by, peers, but channels behaviors in a constructive direction.

The National Academy of Sciences recently reported the first laboratory evidence that cooperative behavior is contagious and spreads from person to person. "When people benefit from kindness they 'pay it forward' by helping others who were not originally involved, and this creates a cascade of cooperation." Authors James Fowler and Nicholas Christakis noted that cooperative behavior cascades in human social networks.

This finding supports the notion of positive peer culture. Knowing that cooperative behavior is contagious leads us to want to seek out the individuals and groups within the organization or community who are already experiencing cooperation. Who has positive communication skills that others trust and want to be around? Who has benefited from a kindness and might be ready to pay it forward? Who is ready to try something new?

The power of positive peer culture was demonstrated in the Youth Leaders of Promise (YLOP) program, a sophomore leadership class the Center developed and taught in the 1990s. Teachers were asked to form a class of students comprised of three types of students:

1) One third existing leaders — students who held visible leadership roles in school government, sports or other activities;

2) One third "diamonds in the rough" or emerging leaders — students who wouldn't necessarily identify themselves as leaders but who, if given encouragement and skills, would emerge as capable leaders;

3) One third clear challenges — students who were clearly influential but displayed their leadership ability in disruptive or negative ways, such as leading gangs.

In the YLOP programs with too many existing leaders, the emerging or challenging leaders were unable to establish their roles, which prevented the spread of the program to the mainstream school population. Programs with too few existing leaders were unable to establish a positive direction and foundered. The most successful YLOP programs had a balance of each type of leader in the class. The even representation of these groupings allowed the development of a positive peer culture that swayed the group toward constructive and inclusive expressions of leadership that lasted well into their junior and senior years.

Adult groups are similar — some individuals are already identified as leaders, some hang back until tapped, and others are seen as disruptive, often because they challenge authority or the status quo. Creating a positive peer group to embrace Gracious Space will go a long way toward activating and sustaining the desired positive changes.

One public agency used three similar categories when selecting members of a leadership program. They invited managers, supervisors, and "leaders at large." This last group consisted of front line employees with leadership potential but without formal authority, and often employees who were disgruntled with policy or management. By engaging these three types of leaders, the program sponsors ensured that the new leadership behaviors and messages would reach a broad cross-section of employees. Program leaders also took advantage of the natural grapevine that exists in every organization to roll out the program. They invited an ad-hoc team of 30 employees from all parts of the organization, especially those known to influence their peers.

They called them the Seed Group, and asked them to review the curriculum and outreach efforts. Not only was this team honored to get the inside scoop before their peers, they became so excited about the curriculum and new direction of leadership, they started gossiping about the program before it launched. They created an optimistic buzz that helped the program gain buy-in with the employees and helped sustain the program for seven years, through three directors, two managers and seven budget cycles.

❖   **Align with a learning or development need.** Often Gracious Space can address a perceived or real gap in teamwork, collaboration or interpersonal communication. Perhaps the community or organization failed to deliver on a promise or goal and is seeking help to do better next time. Perhaps a merger has occurred and people need to let go of their old silos and learn to work with new folks. Organizations conduct satisfaction surveys, or have other means to measure the level of employee engagement and satisfaction. Community groups frequently solicit citizen feedback or invite people to engage in a discovery process or project team. These are opportunities to identify a specific need in the group. Either side of the Gracious Space Change Framework can align with these needs: Opening to Safety, Relationship, Risk or Collective Creativity can help work through an issue; Building Trust, Co-Creating Plans and Purpose, Acting Together, and Sustaining the Work offer steps to address a tangible program need.

Sometimes the group is simply fed up, in despair, or dissatisfied with how things are going. This is a golden opportunity! The psychologist Harry Levinson once observed that if there is not enough pain, a group will not be motivated to move away from the relative comfort of the status quo. Airing the pain felt by group members is often all that is needed to open the group to Gracious Space. What do they have to lose?

In Billings, Montana, some leaders were dissatisfied with their historic inability to reach out to the broad diversity of citizens. Public hearings were attended by the usual suspects, and some city leaders were determined to reach out to more of the community. Led by a champion on the city council, the city developed and hosted a series of dialogues spaced across many months in diverse neighborhoods. They used the principles of invite the 'stranger' and learn in public to hear what people had to say. They created safety and relationship by hosting meetings within different neighborhoods rather than asking citizens to come to city hall. They opened themselves to risk by promising to listen and incorporate ideas into the budget process. They enjoyed collective creativity when the process yielded not only good ideas for a difficult budget, but an inclusive process that made citizens feel heard, seen and honored, and which led to more community engagement in the city's future.

❖ **Align with timing.** Success is often about being in the right place at the right time. A brief review of significant shifts in history reveals that the wheels of change were usually in motion long before results were noticed or an idea took off. The founder of The Body Shop Anita Roddick says, "I am aware that success is more than a good idea. It's timing. The Body Shop arrived just as Europe was going 'green.'"

The story of Rosa Parks is another good example. The myth is that an African American woman decided one day to sit down in the White section of a bus because she was tired, and her arrest started the modern Civil Rights Movement. The truth is that Ms. Parks' action was not the first of its kind. Irene Morgan in 1946 and Sarah Keys in 1955 had won rulings before the U.S. Supreme Court in the area of segregated bus travel. Nine months before Parks refused to give up her seat, 15-year-old Claudette Colvin had refused to move from her seat on the same bus system. But unlike these previous individual actions of civil disobedience, Parks' action sparked the Montgomery Bus Boycott which became an international symbol of racial segregation. Boycott leader Martin Luther King, Jr. then launched to national prominence in the civil rights movement.

Successful change agents are resilient, and bounce back when their timing is off or when they fail. Sometimes we need to put ideas on hold for a few months or years, and keep our eyes open to recognize when the timing is right. Funding becomes available where before it was lacking; a champion emerges where before there was none; a movement takes hold in society or industry that encompasses our change work and gives us the chance to show up.

We introduced Gracious Space to an organization which found the concepts helpful, but didn't take them much further than the first training. A year later, we held a succinct and vibrant review of Gracious Space for a different audience within the same organization, but this time a new leader was in place. She was seeking a way to distinguish her leadership and change the culture, and found the principles of Gracious Space to be exactly what she was looking for. She bought copies of the Gracious Space book for her board and staff and hosted multiple

trainings so that everyone could deepen their understanding and practice of Gracious Space. The second time, the timing was right.

❖   **Leverage existing events and resources.** Groups typically have
events where the introduction of Gracious Space would be natural.
Forums, conferences, staff meetings, team retreats, new beginnings,
transitions, closings, research initiatives and celebratory events are
examples of events that can be used to introduce Gracious Space. By
using existing events and settings, practitioners can avoid making Gracious Space feel like a fifth wheel, or just one more thing people have
to pay attention to. When aligned with naturally occurring events, Gracious Space and the Change Framework can become a welcome part of
the natural cycle.

Resources can also serve as a pocket of openness. Sometimes
funding or personnel becomes available for an effort that matches the
goals of change in the context of Gracious Space. One of our practitioners leveraged her new Executive Director position and budget to introduce the staff and volunteers to Gracious Space. The organization was
the Freedom Project, a non-profit organization that takes mindfulness
training and non-violent communication to Washington state prisons,
and helps ex-prisoners adapt to civilian life.

Compassion was already on Joanne's job description which
delighted her; the office needed to be cleaned and freshened, which
presented an opportunity to focus on the setting of Gracious Space,
and Joanne used staff meetings to introduce her team to her leadership
style and desire to create Gracious Space. She created openings for
safety and relationship, took a risk that employees would accept her invitation, and collectively they better served their clients and volunteers.
"I invited them to help me create an environment where they could
invite the 'stranger' and learn in public together. There was a real release of tension, they were so grateful to be able to express themselves
without fear."

❖   **Choose one or two activities.** Finding the opening for Gracious
Space can be as simple as taking a moment to breathe. It can be taking
a few minutes to inquire about a personal issue that someone is experiencing, or digging more deeply into a comment, rather than letting it
pass unexamined. It can be an invitation for people to speak about an
issue that has been avoided. First steps into Gracious Space have taken
the form of ice cream socials, table toys in meeting rooms, norms for
communication, lunch with the 'stranger,' cross-departmental visits,

team-building retreats, one-on-one mediation and the collective creation of a quilt.

Our experience is that regardless of the group and regardless of the task at hand, people want to connect. They welcome an opportunity to share something that's important to them, or ask questions. If this type of invitation is new to the culture, people may be slow to respond, but once they get into it they will want more. Providing helpful tools is the primary focus of Chapter Ten, but we will share here a couple of examples of how a small activity can be just the opening the group needs.

We recently worked with a small team having some interpersonal communication issues. Three recent altercations between staff had resulted in tears and fear of personal retribution. The team and their brand-new manager started to believe they had vast differences and serious problems to resolve. During a team retreat we introduced Gracious Space, and asked each participant to claim one of the characteristics listed on the Self-Assessment (found at the end of Chapter One).

We then asked them to share that characteristic. Amazingly, out of six people, the group chose only three qualities: being compassionate, being present, and introducing humor. That meant that everyone shared a quality with someone else. This proof of their similarity provided an instant bond and morale boost.

We later did a simple team-building activity called Helium Stick, where the group tries to lower a long pole to the floor without talking. Everyone needs to keep all fingers in contact with the pole and the pole must stay level. Most groups find that the constant upward pressure required to keep their fingers in contact with the pole results in the stick mysteriously rising into the air rather than lowering to the ground. This group managed to lower the stick on the first attempt. It took about two minutes of silent, patient collaboration, but they got it all the way down. When told they were the first in recent history to succeed, they gave each other high fives and jokingly told the facilitator she was no longer needed. These simple activities gave them a direct experience of acting as a high-performing team and they left the retreat believing that's exactly what they were.

After completing the Group Strengths Assessment and identifying potential openings for introducing Gracious Space, change agents will have a better idea of the dynamics that need attention in the group in order to proceed successfully with Gracious Space. A low trust score on the Strengths Assessment, for example, indicates this is a group dynamic that needs to be addressed. A lack of available champions, resources or existing occasions indicates other dynamic issues that need attention if Gracious Space is to be successful.

Open, Neutral or Hard Culture?

Some groups are more ready to adopt Gracious Space as a change strategy. Over the past several years, we've noticed that groups demonstrating trust, compassion, collaboration, and openness to learning, sharing power or trying new approaches are much more open to the Gracious Space Change Framework. The use of Gracious Space in these settings can amplify and focus what's already working. It's also true, however, that Gracious Space has exceptional impact when these elements are lacking and when groups are struggling and ready to try something else.

Assessing readiness for Gracious Space requires an assessment of the environment or culture within which the change is taking place. A culture is simply the spoken and unspoken norms of how things get done. A culture is a system of knowledge or a way of life that people adopt, including behaviors, beliefs, values, and symbols. It is generally accepted without thinking, and is passed along by communication and imitation from one generation to the next.

The good news for change agents is that with intention, culture can be changed. The purpose of this book is to provide a framework for doing just that — to help those interested in collaborative change shift a culture for the good of all. At the same time, Gracious Space is an invitation, not a directive. We need to start where people are, go where it is most open, and apply Gracious Space in ways that fit the group's personality, work and goals.

Now that we have assessed group strengths and identified pockets of openness, it's time to assess the culture of the group and how open it is to Gracious Space. Is the culture open, neutral or closed? How ready is the group to open up? Below is a table that summarizes the characteristics we have been discussing. As with the Group Strength Assessment, start with a group in mind, and assign each issue a rating. The questions in the center can help prompt thinking about different ways the issue may be presenting itself.

Group Readiness Assessment	Some questions to stimulate thinking...	1 (low)	2 (mid)	3 (high)
Safety and Trust	Is it safe? Do we have to be careful? How open and vulnerable are people with each other? Can they ask for help? What is the level of trust?			
Relationships	Do people in the group have genuine compassion and regard for each other? Do they know each other's purpose, passions and gifts? How much do people know about what others do? Are they honest with each other? Is this a happy place?			
Sharing Leadership	How authoritarian is the leadership? Is there a shared vision for the work? What decision making process is most frequently used? Does the group collaborate or protect individual projects or silos? Can this group work together over time?			
Sharing Power	Who wields influence? To what extent is power shared? Do leaders empower and delegate or control and micro-manage? Is there an expert or shared model of leadership? How much fear is present? Does information get shared?			
Communication	Do group members give and receive feedback often and effectively? Is information shared or hoarded? Are there multiple channels for communicating information? Who gives it? Who is left out?			

Group Readiness Assessment	Some questions to stimulate thinking...	1 (low)	2 (mid)	3 (high)
Taking Risk	Is the group willing to experiment and try something new? Is the group willing to run toward the roar, discuss bad news, difficult issues and "elephants in the room?" Is the culture open to taking risks, admitting mistakes and learning from failure? Can the group inquire into judgments, assumptions and patterns?			
Creativity	To what extent are people in the group open to different perspectives? Is the group prone to "group think?" Are there incentives or practices to promote innovation? Can the group hold different perspectives and address conflict respectfully? Can the group stay in uncertainty while creativity percolates?			
Resources and Sustainability	Is the group able and willing to commit time, money and effort to development? Has the group worked effectively through change in the past? Is the group motivated to change? Is the group serious about sustaining their efforts? Do they have a realistic strategy and structure to do so?			
Champions and Peer Groups	Have you found adequate potential champions and peer groups? Will anyone in a position of leadership offer support?			
Awareness of Needs and Existing Occasions	Have you found compelling reasons for change? Are there existing issues that need addressing? Are there natural settings or occasions where Gracious Space can be introduced?			

If the group scores high in most of these categories, then we would say an open culture exists and change agents can dive in! Open cultures are ready and willing to engage in Gracious Space as an extension of what already works for them. They may have a distinct need and are ready to take the challenge. Openness can occur in different ways. Sometimes the leader is open but the people are not; sometimes it's the other way around. Sometimes a department or sub-group is open, but is operating within a more closed or rigid organization or leadership model. The best situation occurs when the top leadership gives full support and there is a culture of trust, strong relationships and willingness to learn and change.

If the group has a lot of middle scores, it's likely the group has a neutral culture. A neutral culture is one where the group is probably open to Gracious Space, but they have developed some unhelpful habits that get in the way. Perhaps they are just too busy, and people in one department no longer understand what others do. They are well-intended, but relationships and communication have dwindled. Perhaps there is a desire for better communication and collaboration, but long-standing social divides such as class or race block their efforts. It's not that a hostile environment exists in neutral cultures, but that they lack frequent and open contact. These groups will likely welcome opportunities for improvement, but finding the appropriate time, place and openings is very important.

If the group scores low in most categories, this can be understood as a hard culture. These cultures are often based on a hierarchical leadership model, a belief in competition and tight control over decision making and resources. Hard cultures do not share power, do not reward risk taking and people within them are understandably reluctant to be vulnerable and try new things. Change agents should proceed with caution in hard cultures and identify openings where a seed can be planted. We do not want to rush to bring the Four Openings and the Four Stages of Change to a toxic environment and end up in a situation where people get crucified for sharing vulnerable information or trying to be more collaborative. However, these are often the cultures that need Gracious Space the most. Many people in these contexts are hungry for more honest and respectful communication. They want an opportunity to level the power dynamics, be themselves, share their gifts and find more life-giving ways to work together.

In hard cultures, practitioners initially may be limited to modeling the elements of Gracious Space in order to find the openings and to find others who want to join in the effort to create a more collaborative and inclusive environment. The reward is held within the practice itself — by modeling Gracious Space, the practitioner can reduce his or her own stress and tension in the middle of difficult circumstances. We have seen this approach work. In very hard environments, Gracious Space is often an act of faith.

A simple way to start the process of creating more openness and leveling power dynamics in hard cultures is to make a request to do something differently. One way to do this is simply to sit in a circle, at the same level. No one person has physical authority in this configuration, and sitting in a circle can subtly reinforce that all voices have equal value. Asking a question and requesting a round robin response during which everyone takes a turn to give her or his thoughts ensures that everyone has a chance to offer a viewpoint. Interrupting patterns of power by asking questions, requesting a break, or asking for time for everyone to write their thoughts and share them are all strategies that can bring more balance to the exchange. These requests require a certain amount of courage in the beginning and may become easier as allies join in making these types of requests. The plan is that, over time, the culture loosens up and Gracious Space takes hold in one or more pockets of openness.

Summary

Assessing and developing readiness includes identifying a group's strengths, defining and beginning to build upon the pockets of openness to Gracious Space, and gauging the overall readiness of the group, community or organization to engage in positive, collaborative change.

Cultures can be open, neutral or hard, but from any starting point change agents can introduce Gracious Space and then expand its application in ever more complete and meaningful ways until it becomes the new culture. We encourage readers to see these assessments as indicators of the most advantageous entry points and differing strategies, rather than a "go or no-go" decision on whether to use Gracious Space. We encourage readers to be bold and courageous in their use of the Gracious Space Change Framework.

Chapter Nine

Case Studies

"It's not what you know, it's what you do with what you know."
—*Unknown*

The introduction of Gracious Space can range from five minutes at the beginning of a meeting to a multi-year process that deepens the capacity of groups to run toward the roar and pursue courageous collaboration together.

There are many reasons to bring Gracious Space into a community or organization. Here are just a few examples of why some groups have introduced Gracious Space:

- To develop new values, vision or mission and identify the behaviors to support those
- As a tone-setter and container for retreats or difficult conversations
- For team building
- To develop new partnerships across departments, organizations, neighborhoods, etc.
- As a mediation approach to address personal or group conflicts and dysfunctions
- To create a safer work environment
- As a way for a new leader or manager to establish a new culture, mission or direction
- As the foundation of a leadership, civic, mentoring or succession planning initiative
- As a stimulus for innovation
- As a framework for a change process

The case studies presented here all share certain elements, regardless of context:

- We first make an initial assessment of where the group is and where they want or need to go. How ready and able is the group to have open and honest conversation? How committed are they to change? How deep are they willing and able to go?

- Next, we recommend starting with an overview of the basic Gracious Space concepts so the group can play with them and make them their own. If the group is hesitant or less receptive, we recommend starting Gracious Space by opening up to the most fundamental behaviors of courtesy and respect.

- Regardless of where the group starts, we create ongoing experiences to practice Gracious Space more deeply over time. Whether the culture begins as open, neutral, or hard, the culture will become more open over time by dedicating time and energy to Gracious Space practices.

"We" refers to facilitators from the Center for Ethical Leadership (CEL). In some case studies, specific activities are mentioned which may be unfamiliar to the reader. In most cases these are explained in Chapter Ten and on the website.

1. A Cultural Shift in a Church Congregation

Audience:

- *Who was the audience?* The congregation and leadership of a church in Seattle
- This was an open culture, in that congregants had an established practice of learning together at an annual retreat, the language of giving an "extravagant welcome" to new people and were willing to learn better ways to communicate and problem solve.
- *How many?* 80 people at the initial retreat, several hundred at subsequent events
- *Why were they there?* Members of the congregation voluntarily attended the retreat and later meetings that applied Gracious Space to discussions of challenging issues.

Goals:

- *What were the goals of the event?* To learn the foundational concepts of Gracious Space; apply inviting the 'stranger;' receive new or different ideas from each other; create space for renewal, relationships and creativity for the members of the church
- *Why were we asked to bring Gracious Space?* Gracious Space was recommended by several congregants already familiar with the principles. The church was in the midst of a profound transition, and anticipated addressing some difficult issues in the coming months, including hiring a new senior pastor. They wanted to foster a more supportive environment to grapple with the issues respectfully and to become a better community.

Initial Assessment:

- *What questions did we ask?*
    - What does success look like?
    - How do we engage the youth?
    - What are you already doing that could be understood as Gracious Space in action?

Way in:

- *How much time did we have?* One evening, one day, one morning (10.5 hrs training time)

- *How did we introduce Gracious Space?* One CEL facilitator designed and led the retreat.

  - In the evening we introduced Gracious Space at table groups by asking each person to bring and describe an object that demonstrated Gracious Space for them; we watched and discussed a DVD called "Celebrating What's Right with the World," by DeWitt Jones and shared a "bedtime" story.

  - The full day began with a 3-hour interactive presentation on the core elements of Gracious Space:

    - ➢ We defined the characteristics of Gracious Space.

    - ➢ We claimed the spirit of the group, which with churches has significant relevance, followed by the Self-Assessment and name-tag activity.

    - ➢ We introduced Invite the 'Stranger,' followed by an exercise of identifying who is the 'stranger' in this group and what the group's patterns are of welcoming those individuals or ideas.

    - ➢ We introduced Learn in Public.

    - ➢ After lunch, the group engaged in a World Café activity to promote learning in public on core church issues selected by the group. After dinner we had improvisational theater games, a children's play and stories.

    - ➢ The final morning featured a discussion on overcoming learned limitations and invited participants to reflect on patterns within the congregation that were no longer serving their goals. They also discussed how to bring lessons back to congregants who were not present at the retreat.

    - ➢ Simultaneously at the regular church worship site, another Center colleague gave a Gracious Space overview and experience to 30 congregants unable to make the retreat.

- *Why did we choose to do what we did?* The congregation was familiar with the church retreat format, and participants came prepared to learn and play together. As there was a history of some people dominating the conversation, we intentionally created ways to invite voices that were not typically heard (youth, elders, quieter members).

Results:

- *How was Gracious Space received?* Gracious Space was readily accepted; the leadership and congregants were very pleased, saying "We want to be sure our new pastor will continue to use Gracious Space."

- *What changes did the group report as a result of their experience in Gracious Space?*

  □ 140 people read the Gracious Space book and discussed it.

  □ They duplicated activities introduced at the retreat into their regular meetings and shifted meeting formats away from lecture to more interaction; Board meetings were re-designed to include more dialogue; planners of the retreat the following year built on Gracious Space and used small group discussion formats.

  □ Subsequent meetings included a review of the basics of Gracious Space, and short stories of where members had seen Gracious Space in action. This built on the work they were attempting and gave a sense of progress and positive change.

  □ Four subsequent conversations on difficult issues were held in Gracious Space over the next year, attended by over 150 people.

  □ A committee formed to make the church more welcoming to diverse individuals.

  □ Leaders felt that they had a positive influence on a substantial shift in church culture, especially learning in public and having more fruitful conversations.

  □ The congregation gained a shared language and sustained the new behaviors to have conversations in a different way.

- *What worked, what would we try differently?*

  □ The light-handed opening during the opening evening program, using real issues during the World Café, playing games on the second evening, involving the young people to express Gracious Space in their own terms, and teaching skills so people felt prepared to have the conversations on their own all worked well.

  □ We could have had more free time during the All Church family camp as there were natural opportunities for conversation while hiking, boating, etc.

2. Staff and Teachers Seeking Cultural Change

Audience:

- *Who was the audience?* Staff and teachers at a coalition of Native American tribes

- This was a hard culture with a pocket of openness in a sub-group. The overarching culture was fairly chaotic and risk-averse, but a sub-group of teachers wanted to create a healthier environment than they were experiencing. They had experience in Native American practices of circle, dialogue and group reflection, and were willing to open up to each other and take risks in a place that didn't reward risk taking.

- *How many?* 20 people

- *Why were they there?* This was a special all-day training to learn how to integrate Gracious Space into their work.

Goals:

- *What were the goals of the meeting?* To learn how to create Gracious Space as a tool for dealing with conflict and experience learning in public together

- *Why were we asked to bring Gracious Space?* The organization had gone through a period of turmoil with changing leadership. Many staff positions turned over. There was increasing recognition that they needed to use more collective leadership to have challenging conversations about important issues in order to help the organization succeed in its mission.

Initial Assessment:

- *What questions did we ask?*
  - How do change processes live in your organization? Is change a process or an event?
  - How would you describe the quality of the relationships?
  - How have you been operating? How do you want to operate?

Way in:

- *How much time did we have?* 9:00 a.m. to 5:30 p.m.
- *How did we introduce Gracious Space?* Two facilitators led the day. The day began with stories of compassion, then facilitators introduced Gracious Space as a tool for bringing compassion into their work. The main steps were:

  - We defined the characteristics of Gracious Space.

  - We claimed the spirit of the place, where there was significant Indian history.

  - We identified the spirit each person brought to this legacy through River of Life stories.

  - We introduced Invite the 'Stranger,' followed by an exercise of Coming to the Center of the Circle, with a discussion of what inhibits welcoming other perspectives.

  - We introduced Learn in Public, followed by a trust exercise of guiding a blindfolded partner.

  - We discussed what people can do to build trust in the organization, and identified conversations they want to have and how to initiate these conversations.

  - We closed with a ceremony asking people what they would commit to as a result of learning about Gracious Space.

- *Why did we choose to do what we did?* We combined experiential activities with reflection and discussion to engage adult learners. Tapping into the spirit of the Native American place was an important source of strength for this organization. It helped focus on relationship building and creating a supportive learning field before discussing the critical issues in the organization.

Results:

- *How was Gracious Space received?* The sponsors readily embraced the concepts, and the group was highly engaged. They saw Gracious Space as a helpful support for conversations. They had some initial ideas about next steps and planned to work with each other to facilitate some of these conversations.

- *What changes did the group report as a result of their experience in Gracious Space?* Individually and collectively in their department they increased their ability to support each other, to take initiative to have conversations important to their work, and to work more collectively. They provided each other with support to navigate the ongoing chaos and relationship dynamics in the larger organization.

- *What worked, what would we try differently next time?* The co-facilitation worked well. It would be helpful to have a specific exercise on how to approach situations of conflict and mistrust. While having a day in Gracious Space provided some impetus and skills for change which was embraced by some staff, the day did not lend itself to long-term change in the overall organization. Having some ownership by the leadership is important to keep the learning alive and gaining traction for long term change.

3. Cultural Shift in a Large Organization

Audience:

- *Who was the audience?* Girl Scout employees working through the merger of many councils into one larger organization

- This group was considered neutral because the new Executive Director was very open to Gracious Space and wanted to lead the group in cultural change, but the group was mixed: some were supportive of making changes and curious about Gracious Space; a few thought the training was a waste of time; the majority were in a neutral place, willing to give it a shot but not necessarily trusting there would be follow through.

- *How many?* 65

- *Why were they there?* This was a mandatory training as part of a two-day department-wide planning retreat.

Goals:

- *What were the goals of the event?* To learn the principles and practices of Gracious Space and bring it into the organization; to create the conditions for meaningful conversations around tough issues on the second day of the retreat; to create agreements about behavior that would support a change in culture

- *Why were we asked to bring Gracious Space?* The Executive Director was familiar with Gracious Space from previous work, and had seen it in action.

Initial Assessment:

- *What questions did we ask?*
    - If this were a very successful day, what would have happened?
    - Who will be in the room and how open are they?
    - What issues are alive in the organization? What is juicy and up for people right now?
    - What are the dynamic issues and conversations the director wants to have on the second day of the retreat, and what is needed to open up the group for those conversations to happen?

Way in:

- *How much time did we have:* One day
- *How did we introduce Gracious Space?* We began with the group silently organizing themselves into a line based on how long they had been connected to the Girl Scouts to get a sense of the history and dedication in the room.
  - We introduced Gracious Space by having pairs tell short stories of a time they experienced Gracious Space, generating a list and discussion of the qualities of Gracious Space.
  - We introduced Spirit, followed by putting a characteristic on their name tag and introducing themselves as that characteristic.
  - We introduced Setting.
  - We introduced Invite the 'Stranger' followed by River of Life activity, where participants drew 3-4 core values that represented them and what they brought to their work. They shared these stories in groups of six people they didn't know very well.
  - We introduced Learn in Public followed by a small-group activity to create a joint image or metaphor that represented the culture they currently had and the culture they wanted to have going into the future. These were posted on the wall followed by a large group debrief to discover common characteristics. The group named the culture they wanted to create together.
  - In the afternoon, we introduced the Four Openings of the Gracious Space Change Framework and individuals completed the diagnostic on where the organization was, followed by a discussion on how similar or different people's perceptions were.
  - We ended the day with an assessment of what they needed to do to move toward their preferred culture and made agreements to move into that culture by work group. The group left with a physical representation of agreements of what they would do to help create the culture they wanted to have.
  - We debriefed which agreements would be organization-wide.
- *Why did we choose to do what we did?* The new Executive Director was very open and wanted to create a new culture. This design brought people gently into a new, shared language, gave them shared experiences over the course of the day to loosen up and build trust with one another, and invited them to explore more deeply their ideas about their preferred culture. It was important to the director to make the shifts tangible and behavioral, so ending with commitments to new behavior that could be measured over time was important.

Results

- *How was Gracious Space received?* Overall it was well received. People embraced the opportunity to make a difference in their own culture — they wanted a good culture and were willing to give it a shot. This was a group that was required to be there (mandatory attendance), and it took a while for some members to warm up to the activities.

- *What changes did the group report as a result of their exposure to Gracious Space?*

  □ The Gracious Space work opened people up for the conversations the next day.

  □ The group improved their skills for having the honest, breakthrough conversations that were needed to discuss how they were going to work together in the future.

  □ They left with physical representations of agreements that they posted in their offices.

  □ In follow-up conversations with the director, she reported people were practicing the agreements and that the shifts people made stayed over time.

- *What worked, what would we try differently next time?*

  □ The most powerful piece was translating an abstract cultural shift (Gracious Space) into meaningful behavioral terms that fit into their own environment, and making agreements to adopt the behavioral shifts that had meaning.

  □ Some questions posed to the group were too abstract and not everyone could connect with them. We could have paid closer attention to getting inside the group's mindset to better understand a specific question that would tap the real juice.

4. Improving Civic Dialogue

Audience:

- *Who was the audience?* Citizens of Billings, Montana
- This was a neutral culture, in that there were several people in the community familiar with Gracious Space, but most of the community was unfamiliar, and some were skeptical that it would be useful or actually change the way things worked.
- *How many?* 100 people
- *Why were they there?* People chose to attend to learn the principles of Gracious Space and be in conversation with their neighbors about important issues.

Goals:

- *What were the goals of the event?* To learn the concepts of Gracious Space (described as hospitable space in the brochure); to join a community conversation on behalf of positive change; to have a greater understanding and awareness of the complexity of community issues; to learn from each other's diverse viewpoints; to come away better prepared to do social and community change; to form new groups committed to working after the event to make progress on an issue they care about
- *Why were we asked to bring Gracious Space?* Several Montana communities had previously hosted a "Can We Talk" conference event hosted by Humanities Montana and featuring Gracious Space. Billings wanted to emphasize the skills of Invite the 'Stranger' and Learn in Public. Organizers wanted this event to be the first of a series of conversations to engage diverse community members in community issues.

Initial Assessment:

- *What questions did we ask?*
    - What does success look like for this day?
    - What balance of up-front presentation and group conversation is desired?
    - What questions will open the group up to creating positive community change?
    - How will you carry the work forward after the event and who will champion that effort?

Way in:

- *How much time did we have?* One day
- *How did we introduce Gracious Space?* One CEL facilitator designed and led the day.

  □ The day began with an introductory keynote on public discourse and community conversations by a well-respected speaker, Brian Kahn, host of "Home Ground," a public radio program.

  □ The morning began with a 3-hour interactive overview of the key concepts of Gracious Space:

  ➢ We introduced Spirit, followed by Self-Assessment activity and writing a characteristic on a name tag and introducing themselves as that characteristic.

  ➢ We introduced Setting, followed by short discussion of what makes a setting welcoming.

  ➢ We introduced Invite the 'Stranger,' followed by individual reflection of a time when they were the stranger and were welcomed in, followed by a large-group call out on what makes it possible to feel welcomed as a stranger. Threesomes then discussed the community's norms around inviting the stranger — what does it look like and what impact does it have?

  ➢ We introduced Learn in Public, followed by the pairs exercise of Two Minutes of Uninterrupted conversation described in Chapter Ten. People could speak for two minutes, responding either to the question "What excites me most about Gracious Space is.." or "What I still don't understand about Gracious Space is.." Then they switched, and we debriefed as a large group what it was like to speak and listen without interrupting.

  ➢ We introduced "World Café" concept. We conducted three rounds of World Café Conversations, with tables facilitated by Leadership Montana members familiar with the ground rules. The questions posed at the tables were: What question, if asked or answered, could make the biggest difference to the community? and What could we do together today that could make the biggest difference to our community? The World Café concluded with a large group report on conversations.

  ➢ We ended by setting a time, date, and place for the first follow-up conversation.

- *Why did we choose to do what we did?* The organizers wanted a balance of inspirational speaking, a presentation of real skills, and the opportunity for participants to use the skills together in real conversations that would help the community move forward.

Results:

- *How was Gracious Space received?* The group embraced Gracious Space and had a good time learning and playing with their neighbors.

- *What changes did the group report as a result of their experience in Gracious Space?*

    ▫ One city council member got very passionate about Gracious Space. She led an initiative to apply the themes of Invite the 'Stranger' and Learn in Public to a three-month citizen-input process, in which city officials unveiled city survey results and sought feedback from citizen groups. Many meetings were held throughout city, in new ways and venues.

    ▫ Three citizens attended a "train the trainer" event to become Gracious Space facilitators.

    ▫ The public library hosted a Gracious Space book club with an introductory video of basic concepts and discussion of the material and potential application.

    ▫ One participant used Gracious Space to facilitate a Food Summit for 50 people with diverse, strong opinions.

    ▫ Another participant brought a CEL Gracious Space facilitator to her family business to foster trust and more positive communication.

- *What worked, what would we try differently next time?*

    ▫ Opening with a respected guest speaker from the local community helped set the need for Gracious Space in their specific context; the World Café conversation format gave people an opportunity to talk about issues that were on their minds.

    ▫ The event sold out; we could have used more space in the room!

COURAGEOUS COLLABORATION WITH GRACIOUS SPACE

5. An Intergenerational Conversation

Audience:

- *Who was the audience?* Youth and the adults who provided human service and leadership development to youth

- This was a neutral culture in that most people involved were unfamiliar with leading group process and did not have previous training in communication skills, but they were enthusiastic about learning and donated their time for the training.

- *How many?* 25, a mix of adults and youth

- *Why were they there?* Participants wanted to learn better ways to communicate across the generation gap. They responded to an open invitation, and attended based on their personal and professional interest.

Goals:

- *What were the goals of the meeting?* To promote intergenerational communication in Gracious Space, so the group could discuss pressing issues in the community and hear from both youth and adults in new ways

- *Why were we asked to bring Gracious Space?* The sponsoring agency was familiar with Gracious Space and believed this approach would be a good context for intergenerational communication.

Assessment:

- *What questions did we ask?*
  - What would it look like if this day was successful?
  - What ways can we shift the training away from adult-centric methods to make sure the youth are comfortable and included?
  - How can we help the adults be comfortable in a format geared more toward youth (experiential, playful, etc.)?
  - What follow-up action do you want the meeting to generate and who will shepherd that effort?

Way in:

- *How much time did we have?* Three hours
- *How did we introduce Gracious Space?* This event was designed and led by a CEL facilitator.
  - We opened with an ice breaker to get people out of their comfort zones (write your name with your non-dominant hand on an index card and hold it to your forehead when you introduce yourself); then we invited the group to tell a story to one other person about someone who helped them when they were a teenager, then as a large group we recalled and listed the qualities of those people.
  - We introduced Spirit, followed by choosing a characteristic of Gracious Space, writing it on their name tag and introducing themselves as that characteristic.
  - We introduced Setting, followed by a discussion of physical settings that invite authentic intergenerational communication.
  - We introduced Invite the 'Stranger,' followed by a short discussion of ways to make someone feel welcome.
  - We introduced Learning in Public, followed by a group activity where small groups discussed one of the elements, what it meant to them and how it could be of value in intergenerational communication, then reported out to the rest of the large group.
  - We did a 10-minute Feed Forward activity to experience Learning in Public. Each person came up with a question they had about intergenerational communication, and posed it to another person. This process was repeated 5-6 times so each person got 5-6 responses to their question in a short amount of time.
  - We held an abbreviated World Café on how to communicate across the generations. World Café questions at table groups included:
    - ➤ What are elements of successful intergenerational work?
    - ➤ What are practical ways we can bring Gracious Space into our work?
    - ➤ What are some ways to build trust and safety in intergenerational work?
    - ➤ What are some of the "elephants in the room" of intergenerational work?
- *Why did we choose to do what we did?* Most workshop formats are designed around adults. To create formats that work for youth, workshops need to include more movement, humor and action. This design incorporated many opportunities for both adults and youth to step out of their comfort zones and try something new.

Results:

- *How was Gracious Space received?* The group readily embraced Gracious Space. They were vocally appreciative and generated animated discussion about how they could use the concepts and practices of Gracious Space in their human service work going forward.

- *What changes did the group report as a result of their experience in Gracious Space?*

  - Several participants brought the principles and skills back to their workplaces.

  - The sponsoring agency was asked to bring Gracious Space to some of the organizations which had been represented.

- *What worked, what would we try differently next time?* The activities that required moving around were helpful to break up the discussion periods. We learned that adults like opportunities to get up and move around, too.

6. Leadership Development in a Retirement Care Organization

Audience:

- *Who was the audience?* A leadership team, consisting of executives, directors, managers and supervisors
- This was a neutral culture in that the leadership was actively supportive of leadership development, yet they knew nothing about Gracious Space.
- *How many?* 34
- *Why were they there?* This was a multi-year leadership development program comprised of mandatory monthly meetings.

Goals:
- *What were the goals of the event?* The goals of the leadership program were to improve personal leadership and effective communication, enhance trust and conflict management skills, establish the practice of mentoring, connect organizational efforts to leadership development.
- *Why were we asked to bring Gracious Space?* Gracious Space was introduced as a shared language and container in which the leadership team could create a learning community and develop leadership together.

Initial Assessment:

- *What questions did we ask?*
  - What are the leadership development needs?
  - Will the program be mandatory or optional?
  - How much trust is there among the leadership team? Does staff trust the leaders?
  - How can Gracious Space best serve this learning community?
  - Who else in the organization needs to know what the Leadership Team is learning?

Way in:

- *How much time did we have:* Three hours every month, for four years

- *How did we introduce Gracious Space?*

  □ The core elements and practices of Gracious Space were introduced in a 3-hour interactive format during the second month of the program, focused on the four core elements of spirit, setting, invite the 'stranger' and learn in public and included:

    ➢ We introduced Spirit, followed by an activity where members shared a time they experienced Gracious Space at the organization and told the story to a small group.

    ➢ We introduced Invite the 'Stranger,' followed by an activity showing the difference between simple, complicated and complex territory, and how to invite diverse opinions when they are dealing in complicated or complex territory.

    ➢ We introduced Learn in Public, followed by a discussion of how to create an open, non-hostile learning environment for the leadership team.

  □ Gracious Space was subsequently introduced to other employees, the board of trustees and the Resident Council.

  □ During the third year of the program, CEL staff introduced a draft version of the Gracious Space Change Framework. The workshop focused on:

    ➢ Telling stories about how Gracious Space was showing up in the organization after one year.

    ➢ Identifying opportunities for Opening to Safety, Relationships and Creativity.

    ➢ Identifying unhelpful group patterns and shifting away from areas of "stuckness."

  □ The organization participated in an Evidence-Based Practice study of Gracious Space.

- *Why did we choose to do what we did?* Gracious Space is an important foundation for learning together. This group needed to develop trust in order to speak openly together and learn new ways to communicate and work together. Gracious Space was just one aspect of a multi-year effort to improve the organizational culture, but set an important tone for the type of leadership the organization wanted.

Results:

- *How was Gracious Space received?* Gracious Space was received well and has become a pivotal cornerstone of how the leadership team works together. Each group that experienced Gracious Space enabled the principles and practices to deepen within the organization and take different shapes. The organization continues to explore and practice Gracious Space four years after the original introduction.

- *What changes did the group report as a result of their experience in Gracious Space?*
  - Gracious Space became common language among staff, board and residents.
  - Mentors and mentees used Gracious Space in their meetings.
  - The leadership program, and Gracious Space, were featured at several annual industry conventions as a "best practice."
  - Participants reported improved trust, communication, collaboration and conflict resolution as a result of their experience in Gracious Space.
  - Participants felt valued and affirmed by the organization's commitment to Gracious Space and leadership development.
  - The leadership team experienced a dramatic cultural change and was able to weather several crises with better teamwork, less negativity and more productivity.
  - The board of directors and executives used Gracious Space to navigate several contentious issues successfully.

- *What worked, what would we try differently next time?*
  - We created small business cards for each participant to give away when they "caught" someone creating Gracious Space; we emphasized different aspects of Gracious Space over time; we invited others in the organization into the discussion, which helped to spread and deepen the experience.
  - It would be helpful to have refreshers on the principles and concepts of Gracious Space, since it is only one aspect of a long term program. It would also be helpful to introduce the Gracious Space Change Framework in its finished form.

7. Mid-South Delta Case

Audience:

- *Who was the audience?* Community members from small towns along the Mississippi River delta in Arkansas. Half of the group was African American and half was White.

- This was an open culture in that the participants were open to learning. However, they were operating within what is historically a very hard culture: in assessing their regional culture, they described themselves as "cautious, traditional, competitive, resistant to change, and distrustful." By agreeing to the leadership initiative, participants demonstrated some openness to working with each other in greater collaboration.

- *How many?* 40 people

- *Why were they there?* They were engaged in an 18-month leadership initiative to work on economic development. Race was the primary dividing issue in the community. The participating communities had previously attempted to work on economic development, and realized that as long as communities continued to be divided by race, they could not make much progress. They needed to create a new "culture of possibilities" that engaged the full talents of both the Black and White communities. To accomplish this required having open, honest, and supportive dialogues about race.

Goals:

- *What were the goals of the meeting?* To learn how to create Gracious Space, and use that foundation to openly discuss race and how to move in tangible ways past its divisive impact.

- *Why were we asked to bring Gracious Space?* They requested Gracious Space because their project coach knew of the impact of Gracious Space in other communities. They purchased books and made them available.

Initial Assessment:

- *What questions did we ask?*
  - Who is this group?
  - How do they want to use or apply Gracious Space?
  - What level of relationship do they currently have?
  - Are there any hot issues that may come up?

Way in:

- *How much time did we have?* One and one-half days.

- *How did we introduce Gracious Space?* There was one facilitator who constructed questions and exercises to draw out participants' stories. Questions were offered in progression from creating an initial invitation and building toward taking more risks.

  - Questions to make them feel safe — build a structure of safety:
    - ➤ When were you the stranger (new to a group) and made to feel welcome?
    - ➤ What are the characteristics of the space that welcomes the stranger?

  - Questions to open up the relationship building and a sense of connectedness:
    - ➤ What do you love most about this place you live?
    - ➤ River of Life activity. What are 4-5 core beliefs and values that guide and inspire you? What are the key experiences that shaped these beliefs and values?

  - Questions to open up to new possibilities:
    - ➤ What are the challenging conversations we need to have in order to create a culture of possibilities?
    - ➤ What do you care so much about that you are willing to work through the uncomfortable conversations?

  - Questions to opening up to your own work:
    - ➤ What happens to you personally when a difficult conversation emerges?
    - ➤ What is your inner thought process and experience when you are at the moment of choosing between closing up and taking risks to speak up?

- *Why did we choose to do what we did?* This region has a long history of racial tension. To help them open up required more than a new technique or identifying next steps in their work together. They needed to connect to their stories and be conscious of the internal experiences they have regarding race. This helped them simultaneously move through an inner and outer work.

Results

- *How was Gracious Space received?* Participants readily embraced storytelling and the concepts of creating Gracious Space together. They welcomed having a supportive way into this difficult area for them.

- What changes did the group report as a result of their experience in Gracious Space?

  - They began to take risks to open up more to each other. They reported that Gracious Space helped them build trust and stronger relationships. One African-American elder woman described herself as a great-great granddaughter of slaves. During the session she held the Gracious Space book in her lap and talked about how much she connected to the concepts. The group continued to struggle with making headway on economic development as 18 months is a short time line for social change.

- *What worked, what would we try differently next time?*

  - The progression of questions and storytelling worked very well in building up their ability to take risks.

  - We could have pressed them more quickly into a dialogue about some aspect of race. There is a big risk that after the Gracious Space facilitator leaves they will play it safe rather than using their safety to have the difficult dialogue. The more they can experience the rewards of such a dialogue early in the process, the better. It is always a question of what the group is ready to do at any given point in the process.

More Success with Gracious Space

There are many examples of how Gracious Space has been used successfully. Here we have chosen a few short accounts from practitioners to demonstrate the range of possibilities for how Gracious Space can be used with impact.

Youth facilitator Mike Beebe: I facilitated workshops for 1,000 Ameri-Corps members serving with Washington Service Corps at a statewide conference. We trained the youth in group facilitation skills. We used the introduction to Gracious Space discussion activity, asking people to form pairs and tell a story where they have experienced Gracious Space. We charted some of the characteristics of those stories, and that led to a really rich discussion of how to integrate different learning styles. They really got that Gracious Space is a space that welcomes different people, different learning styles and inviting the 'stranger,' in whatever form that takes.

Communication and Change Consultant Mark Radonich: As part of a professional development effort for radiation scientists, I wrote a chapter called: "Creating Your Cultural Bridge to Dose, Data, and Scientific Knowledge." This chapter appears in a 2010 textbook entitled Radiation Risk Communication: Issues and Solutions. The chapter focuses on the gap between radiation scientists and non-scientists (aka 'everyone else') in knowing risks of radiation exposure and dose, and suggests frameworks and methods by which both scientists and wider audiences can share their understandings across this often contentious gap. Gracious Space, and specifically the attribute of learning in public, is described as a fantastic framework for scientists to employ, as they seek better and effective ways to communicate and share understandings across educational, organizational, or personal boundaries.

Motivational Speaker and Brain Injury Survivor Lois McElravy: After attending a Gracious Space Facilitator Training, I regularly practiced inviting the 'stranger' so I would feel less sensitive about my brain injury and to gain a deeper understanding about other disabilities. Gracious Space equipped me to effectively participate on boards pertaining to disabilities and opened up opportunities for me to develop and present educational programs for persons affected by disability, including the Montana Governor's Advisory Council for Vocational Rehabilitation and the Montana Association of Rehabilitation (MAR) Conference. Gracious Space has truly transformed my personal and professional lives.

Horizon House CEO Bob Anderson: We had a highly contentious issue regarding our residents' requirement to pay property taxes. Legally they were not required to pay; however, some residents felt it their moral obligation to support state revenues. We framed the issue as a "right versus right" dilemma and stated that success would be defined in the Gracious Space process we used rather than the specific course of action decided upon. Residents and board members listened to each other through four forums and three board meetings plus innumerable emails, letters and bulletins, to better understand the facts, feelings and values underlying the issue. In the end the board voted unanimously to approve the exemption, but also directed a Task Force to meet with residents to facilitate donations in lieu of taxes for those who had interest. This was the most potentially divisive issue in my twelve years here, and in the end, it raised the level of trust in our community. One of the most ardent leaders of the opposition said, "While I am disappointed in your vote, I honor the integrity of the process and the way you conducted yourselves." We practiced the principles of Gracious Space throughout the process and achieved a level of trust within the community that will serve us well in the future.

PTSA Leader: We had a difficult situation in that our new school building was closed due to toxins, and we had to move back into the old building. I wanted to start the year on a good tone with the Parent Teacher Student Association (PTSA), making room for the positive ideas and energy of new parents, without allowing the disgruntlement of old parents to detract from working together. I set up the first meeting in a circle, and described how my children start the day with three minutes of silence. Knowing that adults do not usually take this time, I asked them for one minute of silence, to let go of whatever craziness they had experienced that day and be present. Then I invited each person to introduce themselves with their name, names of their children, and their hopes for the school year. This created a really positive tone. When old negative energy started to creep in, the group would pull the conversation back into a positive direction. At the end of the meeting, two people wanted the same job, and realized they didn't have to compete for it; they agreed to do it collaboratively!

CEL Staff: We facilitated a three-hour Gracious Space training as part of a weekend retreat for a group of Unitarians. Their request was framed in a way that suggested the group was seeking to improve communication skills and that there was no particular issue that needed to be addressed. Since this was an intact group interested in spiritual development, our approach was intended to stretch participants. The group was gradually opened by defining Gracious Space and doing simple spirit and setting activities. Then individuals were asked to reflect on the 'stranger' within and what they could learn by embracing this part of themselves. This reflection was shared in pairs with a very powerful group debrief. For the learning in public element, there was a whole group circle sharing about what each person needed from the group to bring his/her best self to the fellowship. During this round, individuals took great risks to share the ways in which they had felt excluded from participating and the times in which they had felt judged. Individuals made requests for inclusion, understanding and no judgment on the ways that they had failed. It was a very emotional sharing in which every request was wholeheartedly embraced. Later, the retreat organizer shared that some deep underlying issues had surfaced during the Gracious Space training and been addressed during the rest of the retreat. He said that they had made an attempt to address these issues the previous year but it had gone so badly that they had decided to not bring them into this retreat. He was very satisfied with the progress the group made.

CEL Staff: We led a series of conversations on cultural competence and undoing institutional racism for United Way in a large county. The 90-minute conversations were held once a month over the course of one year. We designed and led dialogues in Gracious Space that probed the inner and outer work of undoing racism, including personal beliefs and behaviors, and organizational values and systems. In Gracious Space the group was able to look at their own emotional responses to racism, find ways to be ready with phrases and approaches if faced with racism, animate group conversations where there were existing racist structures, and discuss systems issues to address over time. Gracious Space became explicitly connected with the work of organizations to develop cultural competence and undo racism.

The Impact of Gracious Space

Whether change agents are working in hard, neutral or open cultures, we have seen that Gracious Space can be effective. To add to our anecdotal evidence, the Center conducted an Evidence-Based Practice study to assess quantitatively the benefits of Gracious Space. The people surveyed had received varying amounts of Gracious Space training and were using the core elements (spirit, setting, invite the 'stranger,' learn in public) in different ways to reach organizational and community goals. None had received training in the Gracious Space Change

Framework at that point. When asked about the greatest impact of Gracious Space in their group, the most frequent responses were:

- We are better able to invite the 'stranger' and accept alternate views
- Gracious Space provides more trusting and open communication
- Gracious Space provides a common language, framework and skills
- Our organization or community is more effective because of the use of Gracious Space.

Of 115 surveys returned, a large majority of respondents (83%) said that the use of Gracious Space helped them provide better service within their organization or community and promoted more mindful dialogue and respectful interpersonal communication. Another large majority (75%) said that Gracious Space provided a form of inclusive leadership that got results, and that through the use of Gracious Space they identified patterns that needed to be changed in order to reach their goals. In addition:

- 72% feel very competent or masterful in their ability to learn in community
- 72% feel very competent or masterful in their ability to share power
- 65% feel very competent or masterful in their ability to be open to different perspectives.

These results clearly demonstrate that people who have become trained in Gracious Space enjoy measureable improvements in communication, effectiveness at providing service, the practice of inclusive and result-oriented leadership and greater effectiveness of their organizations and communities. Results also indicate that people who have been using Gracious Space for a period of time have a high level of inner desire to approach leadership collaboratively, and that the practice of Gracious Space enhances that ability.

As noted at the beginning of this Field Guide, the most telling part of the study was the discrepancy between people's ability and confidence to *be* Gracious Space (70%) and their confidence and ability to *do* Gracious Space (23%). Specifically:

- Only 15% feel very competent or masterful in their ability to align Gracious Space to the steps of a change process; 56% feel unable to do this

- Only 23% feel very competent or masterful in their ability to identify and create the appropriate way to bring Gracious Space to a group; 50% feel unable to do this
- Only 23% feel very competent or masterful in their ability to draw out learnings and milestones for groups during their process; 44% feel unable to do this.

The results demonstrate that people need more information about how to "operationalize" the principles and concepts of Gracious Space into practical facilitator tools, meeting activities and change processes. They need a tool box to support their work, and the confidence and experience to know how to apply the tools toward a specific goal over time. These are the areas we address in this book, especially in Part Two, and particularly in the next chapter on Tools and Activities to Establish Gracious Space. Complete results of the Evidence-Based Practice study can be found on the Center's website at www.ethicalleadership.org.

With all of the successes of various groups in bringing Gracious Space to life, we need to acknowledge that the Center and our practitioners certainly have examples where the introduction of Gracious Space didn't work very well. Gracious Space isn't a panacea for all that ails individuals, groups or systems, and there are times when it simply doesn't land well. The reasons for this vary, but typically are related to lack of ownership or investment from the top, and/or a hard culture that resists collaborative learning.

In these situations that "fail," we have tried to be open about our own learning in public. We review the sessions and try to identify the factors that made the sessions ineffective so that we can better work with these factors in the future. Having a peer group of practitioners helps in the debriefing process so that even in the midst of what appears to be failure, there is learning. We also believe that seeds can be planted even during a disappointing gathering, and some individuals or the group may go in a slightly different direction because of their experience in Gracious Space. We may never know about those shifts. Gracious Space is often an act of faith — faith that the ripples of learning extend far beyond our ability to discern or measure.

Summary

Les Brown once said, "You don't have to be great to get started, but you have to get started to be great." Each of these case studies demonstrates that courageous people in vastly different settings have successfully introduced Gracious Space to their communities, workplaces and organizations in many different ways. The positive benefits outweighed the uncertainty or fear they initially experienced, and in most cases, Gracious Space continues to deepen in those organizations and communities.

We invite change agents preparing to introduce Gracious Space to use the template we followed in the case studies to determine their audience, make an assessment through good questions, prepare a design and "ways in," and evaluate the results. We look forward to hearing about your experiments and successes!

Chapter Ten

Tools and Activities to Establish Gracious Space

"Action will remove the doubts that theory cannot solve."
— *Tehyi Hsieh*

The process of creating Gracious Space — where in a spirited setting of trust and acceptance we welcome the 'stranger' and encourage learning in public — requires both being and doing. Gracious Space is a state of mind and heart (being), and also comprises a set of tools and activities that we engage in (doing) to open people up for learning together.

This chapter shares many ways to establish Gracious Space. Some are simple and can be done without a lot of fanfare; others are more extensive and are designed to take a group deeper. These tools include the creative use of questions as well as activities that can activate the four basic elements, the Four Openings and/or the Four Stages of Change. Many of the activities can be used for multiple purposes, and can be combined in different ways to design a meeting, half day workshop, multi-day retreat or longer-term process.

Practitioners of Gracious Space have used these and many other activities to establish Gracious Space in very diverse groups. Most of these activities are, at first glance, merely a series of steps. If achieving transformational and collaborative change were simply a matter of following a series of steps, we'd all be in a much better place much more easily. There is a slippery, unpredictable magic that happens when people interact with a design or an activity — something that transcends the activity as written. An even more slippery magic has to occur for that good result to last and increase over time.

Can we name that slippery magic? Can we bottle it? Can we guarantee it will occur each and every time? Unfortunately, no. But we can support the relational field, make the invitation to Gracious Space, create the conditions and bring our best intentions for a good outcome. Certainly, trying to consistently match the activities to the group contributes to a positive group experience. And, there is something powerful about repetition — about continuing to learn and to practice. Positive results sometimes take longer than we wish and come back around in ways we can't see or predict in the moment.

Start with What You Know

The seeds of Gracious Space lie within all of us. The seeds lie closer to the surface in some people and more deeply buried in others. An invitation to Gracious Space, through any activity, will invite people to bring their innate capacity for Gracious Space more fully to the surface of their lives and work. When people come together and form a unique relational field, they can collectively draw on and deepen their capacities for Gracious Space within that field, which, in turn, allows them to deepen their work over time.

When it comes to "doing" Gracious Space, practitioners should feel welcome to bring their own approaches to the work. We suggest practitioners identify which interactive approaches they already have at their disposal or have already mastered. This process usually helps practitioners realize they know more than they thought they did about how to establish Gracious Space. For example, perhaps a practitioner is trained in mediation, or dialogue, or circle process. Perhaps a manager has used an icebreaker that reliably builds safety and trust in a group. Perhaps a practitioner is familiar with World Café, Open Space Technology, Appreciative Inquiry or another large-group learning process. Knowledge of any activities like these is an entry point to apply your own approaches to the doing part of Gracious Space. The Competency Worksheet at the end of Chapter One can help practitioners identify which interactive approaches they already have at their disposal or have already mastered.

Once practitioners have identified the approaches they already have at their disposal, the next step is to evaluate how a specific approach might work with the various Openings and Stages of Change. The following questions can assist in this discernment.

- Which activities and experiences generate personal safety within the group? Which behaviors and actions compromise safety?

- Which activities generate trust in a group?

- Which activities or experiences produce deeper relationships that are open to learning, inviting of difference and willing to explore individual and group habits and patterns? Which cause relationships to falter or wither?

- What project-planning tools can help groups co-create their shared purpose and plans?

- What experiences or supports can help groups tread into areas of risk and discomfort? What fears could shut down the imagination? What would happen if the group failed to venture into this capacity? What would happen if it did?

- What groups are acting together over time? What experiences or activities help them to stay together in the work? What is likely to drive them apart or threaten the work?

- What are the hallmarks of collective creativity? What activities, experiences or tools enable groups to be in an extended space of shared creativity? What blocks creativity?

The Importance of Good Questions

Einstein was once asked what he would do if he were given an hour to solve a problem. He replied that he would spend the first 55 minutes defining the question, and after that the answer would likely be obvious! Most of the problems we face in our communities and organizations take longer than an hour to resolve; but Einstein's advice still holds. Defining the question is one of the most potent leadership tools available.

The Center believes that the ability to ask a good question is a hallmark of transformational leadership, and the Gracious Space Change Framework is constructed on the belief that, generally, a good question is more powerful than a good answer. Every change process advances in its own way, influenced by the particular context and what the group's experiences have been. The Framework's components of the Four Openings, Four Stages of Change and the Inner Work of the Change Agent and Group provide guidelines and questions to help a group perceive where they are in their change work and navigate what is next. By asking questions that stimulate curiosity, catalyze new ideas or require a shift to perspectives that weren't considered previously, the group confronts complexity, moves through the components of change and accelerates its learning.

Good questions are of true benefit no matter where the group or organization is in the change process. Good questions provoke new and deeper modes of thinking and sensing, and open up completely new vistas of possibility. True enough, good questions can sometimes cause discomfort because they ask us to confront that which we would prefer to ignore. Questions that make us uncomfortable because they challenge us are not to be confused with questions that are uncomfortable because they are self-defeating and shut people down, thwarting healthy individual and group passion, spontaneity, and involvement. We want to avoid questions that are merely rhetorical or are solely intended to make a point (Why didn't you know that beforehand?) or to lay blame (Who is responsible?).

In general, questions which are genuinely thoughtful, positively focused, and empathetic in nature serve to open people up and help us move through the change process. Examples include:

- What is your story?
- What matters?
- Who else cares?
- What is working?
- What is possible?
- Where is it open?
- Who has resources?
- What do you need or want in order to stay involved?
- What do you need or want to let go of for the sake of the whole?
- What will help us be our best?

Asking these questions helps us learn meaningful data relevant to the change process, opens up curiosity to hear new perspectives and engages people at deeper levels.

Forming Compelling Questions

There is another purpose for questions, and that is to set the direction for the work that will be done. We call this kind of question a compelling question. A compelling question is one that engages a group in deeper learning and transforms its understanding of an issue. Forming a compelling question requires us to name the inherent (and sometimes opposing) values within an issue, and then craft a question that blends, bridges and builds on those values, with enough possibility to create direction and enough specificity to create traction.

The use of compelling questions can open a group up to profound transformation and learning. Facilitator guides for helping a group discover compelling questions are available on the Gracious Space Practitioner's website, and a brief description is in the Handholds section of this chapter.

Some examples of compelling questions follow. The inherent values that got embedded through blending, bridging and building are underlined:

- A school was deciding whether to keep the image of an American Indian as its mascot. Young Indians identified with the image and felt proud, and Whites liked the tradition, but older Native Americans felt offended. Their compelling question: *How can we have a mascot that builds strong community and identity for all of us?*

- A community group was addressing its energy needs for the future. Dams had been opened up, contributing to the loss of cheap energy. A coal plant could move in, but some citizens were seeking new, cleaner alternatives. Their compelling question: *How do we take charge of our energy future while protecting the environment from unmonitored development and retaining our sense of a small and friendly community?*

- A community group was trying to transcend a decade-long debate about traffic. Their compelling question: *How can the city integrate safe, shared roadways with quiet and clean neighborhoods while maintaining efficient, cost-effective traffic flow for commercial and residential use?*

- An organizational leadership team was considering its goals for the coming year. With economic cutbacks, loss of employee morale and a need to give leaders the skills to be effective in complex and uncertain territory, their compelling question was: *How do we deepen trust and communication while engaging in community service and generating shining eyes in our employees?"*

- A newly formed leadership team was seeking to create a values-based structure to guide their decision making and program priorities for the coming years. Their compelling question: *"How do we deliver results on justice and advocacy, while communicating openly and working collaboratively with our membership?"*

When we discover the question that excites people and points to an obvious and positive direction, we are better able to inform what will happen next in ways that expand possibilities. One mayor, after seeing a list of compelling questions a group of citizens had assembled, commented with deep feeling that this type of question was a revelation. "These questions make me want to sit down with you and answer them, rather than roll my eyes at the same old posturing that typically happens in community discussion."

Using Questions to Open People Up

There is a final aspect of asking questions that we want to make explicit — asking questions can help move a group to the next level. As a group moves through a process, an effective practitioner will develop and offer a series of questions or activities that move the group gradually into deeper and more difficult territory. Posing increasingly challenging questions invites the group to share with each other in a way that is more gracious than diving in cold all at once.

In every exchange, Opening to Safety and Opening to Relationship require attention before moving to Opening to Risk. Here is an example of a progression of questions designed to lead participants to a deeper conversation, in this case, on the role of racism in society:

- What was shared with you the first time someone talked to you about race?
- What happened when you first experienced a difference between you and others related to your racial or ethnic background?
- If you have witnessed or experienced an act of racism, what did it do to your spirit or your sense of wholeness?
- What helps you to come to a place of wholeness after you have experienced or witnessed acts of racism?

In the section that follows, practitioners can consider which activities are naturally aligned to different stages of deepening the work. In a number of these activities, there are choices for framing the activity or selecting questions to ask. It is always helpful to consider readiness and the group's current conditions in making those choices.

30 Handholds into Gracious Space

In this section, we share 30 ways to help establish Gracious Space in groups, ranging from low-risk to high engagement. In parenthesis we have noted which aspects of the Gracious Space Change Framework the activity most directly enhances. In most cases, more detailed instructions can be found on the Center's Gracious Space Practitioners page at www.ethicalleadership.org. It is important to use different modalities such as movement, art and humor to engage the full spectrum of intelligences, instead of being limited by just one approach. Experiential learning integrates playful moments with serious work, with the goal of being light without being artificial. If we can get people to loosen up, relax, perhaps even to laugh at themselves, they will be more ready to engage with new ideas and learn in public.

1. **Three Breaths.** (Spirit) You can do this as a self-preparation exercise on your own, or you can involve others. Sounding a gong or bell at the beginning of the breathing exercise is a helpful indicator that something new is happening. The physiological act of breathing brings more oxygen to the brain, which has been shown to make people more alert and have better reactions. Here is a sample progression for a breathing routine: On the first breath, ask people to focus on letting go of any tension, craziness or concerns they experienced prior to gathering; on the second breath, ask them to become present in this space and with these people; on the third breath, ask them to imagine the gifts they can bring to the work at hand. At the end of breathing, remind participants that they can ask for a pause or a breath in the proceedings at any time.

2. **Bring an Object that Represents Gracious Space.** (Spirit, Setting, Build Trust, Open to Safety, Open to Relationship) Prior to the meeting or event, ask members to identify and bring an object that represents Gracious Space to them. Items vary widely — from a photograph of a place or person, to an object of beauty or inspiration, to a poem — but all the offerings have value for the bearer. These items can be shared in a large group, with each person taking a turn to place an object in the middle of the circle while describing it. If the group is very large or the time is short, the sharing can be done in small groups, followed by a large group discussion that

invites a few of the items to be shared. Small groups could also be followed by a process of each person simply stating the characteristic the item represents, such as "beauty," or "listening," and placing it in the center of the circle. Having the items displayed in the center creates a visual, tangible, powerful, and sometimes sacred, gallery of the characteristics of Gracious Space, which the group can refer to during their time together.

3. **Tell a Story.** (Build Trust, Open to Safety and Relationship) The use of stories is a heartfelt way to open a group to experience more trust and relationship. The invitation to tell a story creates an opening for participants to learn about each other, share something that is important to them, and find their voice at the beginning of a meeting or process. The particular story can vary depending on the circumstances of the group. Some of the invitations we have made include: Tell a story of a time you experienced Gracious Space; of a time you were held with compassion; of a time you were welcomed as the 'stranger'; of a time the group performed at a high level of trust or performance; of a time you had a difficult conversation that went well. We typically ask people to tell stories to one or two other people, giving them about 5-10 minutes to share. We then ask participants to describe the characteristics that were present in the stories, such as "welcoming," or "vulnerability." Making a list of these characteristics can lead to a discussion on norms, and how the group wants to be together.

4. **Self-Assessment/Name-Tag Activity.** (Spirit, Build Trust, Open to Relationship) Ask people to complete the Gracious Space Self-Assessment (found at the end of Chapter One), selecting a handful of characteristics they feel are naturally part of their own gifts of Gracious Space. They can also identify one or two characteristics they would like to improve. Facilitators can invite participants into small groups to discuss these aspects, and invite them to hold each other accountable for bringing their gifts and working on their areas of improvement. Then ask them to select one characteristic for the purposes of this day, this meeting, or this time, which they feel particularly strong about right now. They write this characteristic on a sticky name-tag and attach it to themselves. Ask people to mill around the room, introducing themselves as that characteristic. For example: "Hi, I'm being compassionate." "Hi, I'm willing to change my mind." This activity generates positive and sometimes loud energy, encourages people to publicly claim their gifts, and helps form a positive relational

field in minutes. Several people will likely share the same characteristic, which helps them find their buddies. People often refer to
their characteristic during the remainder of the meeting, a habit
which begins to establish the shared language of Gracious Space
and being accountable for its creation. Participants can be asked
to intentionally bring these gifts to bear on whatever discussion or
decision is at hand.

5. **Group Agreements.** (Build Trust, Open to Safety) The goal of this
   activity is to generate an agreed-upon list of noble behaviors the
   group will commit to during their time together. Forming group
   agreements can build on any exercise that harvests characteristics
   of Gracious Space from stories or inquiries. Once the list of desired
   norms, behaviors or characteristics is assembled, facilitators can
   ask if there are any characteristics missing (often, confidential-
   ity or fun) that would make people feel safe in this space, and
   add those to the list. Too often, establishing group norms takes
   a "lowest common denominator" approach, where we agree on
   the floor of behaviors below which we won't go. In contrast, this
   approach asks people to commit to reaching high and bringing
   their best stuff while they are together. The list of agreements can
   be referred to during the meeting as reminders or as requests by
   anyone who feels the agreements are not being met.

6. **Something We Can't Tell by Looking.** (Build Trust, Open to Safety,
   Open to Relationship) A facilitator invites participants to write on
   an index card one true thing about themselves the others can't tell
   by looking. Encourage people to put down something outrageous
   they have done or which has happened to them, and which they
   want to share. Put the cards in a basket. Throughout the group's
   time together, someone pulls a few cards, reads them, and the
   group tries to guess who it belongs to. This can be done at various
   times throughout a meeting to provide a break and enable people
   to get to know each other in a fun, personal and safe way.

7. **Things We Have in Common.** (Build Trust, Open to Safety, Open
   to Relationship, Co-Construct Shared Purpose) Participants form
   5-7 groups and within their group discover five things they have
   in common in two minutes (nothing obvious like, "we're all in this
   room"). Then they form three larger groups and discover three
   things they have in common with that group. Lastly, they form
   one big group and discover one thing they all share in common.
   The debrief shows that even though participants come from differ-

ent backgrounds, there is at least one thing they have in common. This forms a basis for safety and for doing shared work.

8. **Assessing Common Ground.** (Build Trust, Open to Safety, Open to Relationship, Open to Risk, Open to Collective Creativity, Co-Construct Shared Purpose and Plans, Learn in Public) "Are we ready, and do we have sufficient common ground and trust upon which to stand and work together?" This is an important question to be explored before embarking on any group venture. It is prudent to ensure that there are reasonable conditions for success before spending time and valuable resources. Ask participants to reflect on two questions: "What does a successful outcome look like?" and "What do I really care about and am committed to?" The first question clarifies intent and purpose. The second question surfaces core values. Give a few minutes for participants to write their answers, then invite each person to share their reflections with no interruption from others. After everyone has spoken, begin an inquiry to discover what participants mentioned in common. List these on a visible chart under the heading "convergence." Repeat the process, inviting comments that illustrate differences, and title this list "divergence." Ask the group whether there is sufficient common ground to begin the work, based on this conversation. If they agree to move ahead, ask people to commit to figuratively carrying both lists. At each subsequent meeting, review the lists to see if the common ground is holding, and whether any items on the divergence list have moved over to form an aspect of convergence. This activity was introduced by Michael Lindfield.

9. **Assessing Trust.** (Build Trust, Open to Safety, Open to Relationship, Open to Risk, Invite the 'Stranger,' Learn in Public) Trust is a vital ingredient in the psychological soil of group life and its presence creates the conditions that allow us to lower our defenses and wholeheartedly enter the vulnerable space of learning and growth. This activity helps to establish trust by thinking about three elements of trust: a) Character — a person or group's basic personality and way of being in the world. Do they possess a good, true character? b) Competence — the degree to which the person or group is capable of doing their part, or job. Do they have the right skills and expertise? Do they have relevant and good ideas about the work? Can they plan and implement the work competently? and c) Consistency — the reliability of a person or group, and their results. Is this person or group reliable and accountable? Do they follow through on good ideas? Are they consistently present and competent? Ask

participants to identify the areas in which a person or group is or is not trustworthy (this can be done anonymously). Assign a numerical value, such as 1-5, for the amount of trust present. If the trust level is 4 or above, it is probably safe to proceed. If the level of trust is 3 or below, this indicates more inquiry and trust building are needed. This activity was introduced by Michael Lindfield.

10. **Come to the Center of the Circle If.** (Build Trust, Open to Relationship, Invite the 'Stranger') This activity helps identify the 'strangers' among us and can be used as the starting place for a conversation around the 'stranger.' The group stands in a circle. A facilitator reads a number of prepared statements, and invites people to move to the center of the circle if the statement is true for them. Once people have moved inside, they pause for a moment to see who else is there, then return to the outer circle. Use a variety of statements, which can become increasingly personal and/or provocative. For example: "Come to the center of the circle if you are a parent; if you grew up here; if you are under the age of 30; if you or someone close to you has had cancer; if you or someone you know has gone hungry; if you have a close friend of a different race." Statements can also reflect the topic at hand, such as: "Come to the center of the circle if you have been an activist; if you have participated in a political campaign; if you have led a successful work team; if you know a victim of youth violence; if you have spoken out against a racist comment." When the facilitator finishes, he or she can invite group members to name additional statements they want to mention in the circle.

11. **Yes, And.** (Spirit, Invite the 'Stranger,' Learn in Public, Open to Relationship, Open to Risk, Open to Collective Creativity) This improvisational theater game gives people practice with the posture of accepting an offer and building on it. It is a good warm-up for inviting the 'stranger.' Demonstrate one round and then have the rest of the group do the activity in small groups of 5-7. Have groups stand in a circle. One person starts a story with a sentence or two. The story can be random, silly and fictional or more serious and related to the topic. For example, "On my way to the meeting today, I was bit by a dog wearing a purple hat." Or, "One day a 'stranger' came to my meeting and asked if he could join us. He was a Republican, I am a Democrat." The next person in line accepts the story by saying, "Yes, and...," continuing the story from where the previous speaker left off. This repeats until the very last person, who brings the story to a (somewhat) logical close. The debrief usually demonstrates

that participants had to be fully open to the storyline and could not decide ahead of time what they would say, because the story would inevitably change by the time it was their turn! This is a fun activity that generates positive energy and gets people into a physical and mental state of being open to surprise and accepting new ideas.

12. **Being in Circle.** (Spirit, Build Trust, Open to Safety, Open to Relationship, Invite the 'Stranger') Being in circle is a powerful way of tapping into and strengthening personal connections and relational intelligence. Circle work can be done at many levels, and can build on traditions a family, community or organization is already familiar with. Circle processes can create openness, invite deeper sharing and level power dynamics. Briefly, people sit in chairs arranged in a circle so everyone can see everyone else. A question or discussion point is identified and people are invited to respond, each taking a turn and going around the group. A time limit can be set to monitor people's responses, or it can be left open within a general boundary (such as, we need to be done by 10:00). It may help to start with a moment of silent reflection for people to jot down what they wish to say. This way they will feel prepared, and will be fully present to listen to others speak. One truth about circle seems to be that as the conversation makes its way around the group and more is shared, people toward the end become tempted to build on and bridge with what has come before, which leads to more lengthy responses. It is important to create a sacred or safe space for the circle process, otherwise participants will not feel safe enough to be vulnerable, and the process may feel like "circle-lite." For information on practicing deeper Circle work, we recommend The Little Book of Circle Processes: A New/Old Approach to Peacemaking, or Peacemaking Circles: From Crime to Community, both by Kay Pranis.

13. **Blindfold Walk.** (Invite the 'Stranger,' Build Trust, Open to Relationship, Open to Risk) This is an active exercise that encourages team building and the immediate development of trust. One person puts on a blindfold and allows another person to lead them to a specific destination, then they switch places for the return journey. Debrief questions can include: What was it like to trust someone and how much risk were you willing to take based on that trust? What was it like to be responsible for someone and how did that change your normal behavior? There has to be enough trust already present in the group to do this activity.

14. **Pose a Series of Questions.** (Invite the 'Stranger,' Build Trust, Open to Risk, Learn in Public) Pose a series of questions that invite participants to share gradually more revealing information, first facts, then opinions and beliefs, then emotions. By increasing the risk over time, facilitators will find that when participants can answer more simple questions first, they are more likely to answer the more challenging questions toward the end. Here is a series asked of business managers experiencing low morale and trust:

- What is your job? (fact)
- What attracted you to this work place? (fact/opinion)
- Why do you stay? (fact / belief)
- What values are important to how we work together? (beliefs/ emotions)
- What do they look like? (beliefs/ emotions)
- How much trust do you feel in this organization? (emotion)

The organizer needs to do something with the information revealed. The activity will build trust, but also requires trust to steer the information shared into helpful insights and decisions about how to move forward.

15. **Blocks Game.** (Work of the Change Agent and Work of the Group, Open to Relationship, Open to Risk, Invite the 'Stranger,' Learn in Public) This non-verbal game requires very little set up, just a bag of building blocks (such as wooden ones used by children) and instructions. The group sits in a circle so everyone can see each other and the central floor area. The instructions are: 1) each participant will take a turn, going in a circle, 2) each person moves one block at a time, 3) there is no talking, and 4) it's over when it's over, meaning the group has to nonverbally decide how to end the game. People typically follow the rules for a few rounds, but then someone takes a risk by stretching or breaking the rules — this is the point of the activity. For example, someone might move a block completely out of the circle or give it to someone. Someone might move more than one block, go out of turn, or use a block to destroy something that has been created. When people start breaking the rules, participants will have different reactions. Some will quickly liberate themselves from the rules and dive in; others may retreat and even be offended. The gem in this exercise is uncovering patterns: participants' reactions often mimic how they usually show up in other group settings. The debrief can explore rule following and rule breaking, who leads, who observes, how they relate to others

within groups, what they might need to let go of to be in service to the whole, and what they need from others to stay engaged.

16. **Milling Exercise.** (Build Trust, Open to Relationship, Open to Risk, Invite the 'Stranger') Introduced by Joanna Macy and Molly Young Brown in <u>Coming Back to Life</u>, the Milling Exercise is active and nonverbal, and provides a change of pace after people have been sitting and talking. People move about the room silently, pausing periodically at the facilitator's invitation to stand before another person. The facilitator then asks each person to imagine something about the person standing before them: such as their skills and beauty, pain experienced, or future potential. Confronting one another's joys and pains often jolts hearts and minds open more quickly and powerfully than words, and breaks open our capacity to care and collaborate. We recommend this activity be used after some comfort and trust has been built, such as the second or third day of a retreat or after the group has met a few times. A debrief is important to allow people to express the impact this activity has on them.

17. **Carousel Brainstorm.** (Invite the 'Stranger,' Learn in Public, Co-Construct Shared Purpose and Plans, Open to Collective Creativity) This activity introduces movement into a brainstorm process and underscores the collective wisdom in a group. It can be modified to achieve a variety of learning purposes. A facilitator identifies 4-5 questions or discussion themes, and writes each one on a separate sheet of easel paper. For example a carousel brainstorm could be around group patterns: What are some common patterns in groups? What are ways to identify patterns? What are ways to reinforce positive patterns? What are ways to shift away from unhelpful patterns? The papers are posted at different spots throughout the room. Small groups form, and take turns visiting each flip chart and adding comments and insights about that specific question. After about 5-10 minutes, groups move to the next chart, like a carousel. It helps if each group uses a different colored marker to identify their contributions on the chart. Each group arriving subsequently reads the previous offerings, and builds on them. The activity concludes by having groups return to their starting point, summarize key points and report back to the large group the key lessons or ideas.

18. **Twelve Solutions.** (Invite the 'Stranger,' Open to Collective Creativity, Sustain the Work) Introduced by Bruce Takata, this exercise asks participants to identify an issue they are grappling with, and then find twelve possible solutions to that issue. It can be done individually by asking people to focus on a particular challenge or habit they want to change, or as a group. Ask people to silently write the solutions down as fast as they can. At first, they will likely come up with conventional ideas, but gradually they will move beyond those to a more creative arena. A practice round can be done to help the group warm up to creative thinking. For example, we once asked table groups to put someone's shoe in the center of the table, and generate as many uses for the shoe as possible in two minutes. Then we moved to an issue more related to the topic at hand, which in this case was ways to invite the 'stranger' to their community. For the second round, we gave more time to generate ideas and process their creativity.

19. **Overcoming Learned Limitations.** (Invite the 'Stranger,' Learn in Public, Open to Risk, Open to Collective Creativity, Act Together, Sustain the Work, Work of the Change Agent, Work of the Group) A learned limitation is a habitual pattern of thought or behavior that once served but now often does not. It limits our adaptability or effectiveness in a given situation. This can be true both for individuals and groups. Ask participants to sit with one other person. Ask them to take five minutes in individual silent reflection to examine a time when they transcended a learned limitation, either a personal limitation or a group limitation. How did they recognize the pattern, how did they interrupt it, how did they create a new pattern, what was the resistance? What worked, what didn't work? At the end of five minutes, share reflections in pairs, taking five minutes each. Reconvene in the large group to share learning by addressing the question: "What made transcending this learned limitation possible?" Capture ways to identify and interrupt patterns of stuckness. More information about learned limitations can be found by referencing the work of Dr. Milton Erickson. This activity was introduced by Bruce Takata.

20. **Feed Forward.** (Invite the 'Stranger,' Learn in Public, Open to Risk, Open to Collective Creativity) This activity resembles "speed dating" and enables participants to generate many ideas in a short amount of time. The group forms two concentric circles, with the inner circle facing out, and the outer circle facing in. One circle is called "A" and the other circle is "B." Each person is asked to form

a question or identify a curiosity they have around a central theme. It could be about leadership, or about a topic they are engaged in. Taking turns, people in circle "A" pose their questions to the person facing them in circle "B," who answers it as best they can in one minute. After one minute, they switch, with people in circle "B" posing their questions to their partner in circle "A," who also has a minute to respond. Then the inner circle moves one space which gives each person a new partner. Repeat the process, with people asking their same question of the new person across from them. Repeat 5-6 times. Debrief questions can include: What it was like to speak for a minute without interruption? To listen for one minute without interruption? What did you learn from asking the same question of multiple people? What was it liked to be asked?

21. **Stop, Start, Continue.** (Open to Risk, Open to Collective Creativity, Co-Construct Purpose and Plans, Act Together, Sustain the Work) This is a brainstorming activity where the group considers three aspects of their work: 1) what they want to *stop* doing because it is not working, not helpful or outdated; 2) what they want to *start* doing because it will contribute positively to the task or process; and 3) what they want to *continue* doing that is already working for them. Responses could include individual and group behaviors, norms, practices, work systems or policies. Identifying these three areas gives groups an opportunity to reflect on the helpful and un-helpful patterns of their work, and make changes to support their growth and productivity. The results can serve as the beginning of a strategic plan or mission statement.

22. **Core Values Exercise.** (Build Trust, Open to Safety, Open to Rela-tionship, Invite the 'Stranger,' Co-Create Shared Purpose and Plans) This activity is one of the core foundations of the Center's curricu-lum, and can be used in a variety of settings where it is important to discover and claim the values of participants. The exercise is challenging, and is more meaningful if people do it silently on their own. Give participants the list of Core Values (which can be found on the Center's website). Ask them to review the list, and add any values that are important to them that are not shown. From here, we reduce the list. Be sure to emphasize participants are not *throwing values away,* but rather, are making relative choices. It is important to give people ample time to make their selections. Ask participants to narrow their list to eight values, then to five, then to three, and finally to two.

Ask them to pay attention to their inner dialogue as they do this. The narrowing process typically takes about five to ten minutes.

At the end of the selection process, invite participants to stand, state their name, and state their two core values. This gives a sense for the unity and diversity in the group. From here you can invite participants into small groups to discuss why and how they selected these values, what they mean to them, and how they act on them. Facilitators can determine the shared values of the group by adding a second part to the exercise. State one of the most frequently mentioned values (usually love, family, integrity) and ask people to stand and remain standing if that is one of their top two. State another value that was frequently mentioned, and another, until all are standing. If one or two people had unique values and are still sitting, facilitators can ask which of their own values they wish to stand for at this moment. Write all values on a flip chart so people can see the values they stand for together. This list of shared values can become the starting point for building common ground or purpose. A detailed self-guided Core Values Exercise is located on the Center's main webpage.

23. **River of Life.** (Build Trust, Open to Safety, Open to Relationship, Invite the 'Stranger,' Learn in Public) This story-telling activity invites people to think of different phases of their lives, and represent those visually in a drawing. Facilitators should first identify a key question or theme, such as a leadership development path, their life as an activist, etc. Ask people to create a picture that reflects the river of their lives, including the bends, whitewater, eddies or joining tributaries that impacted their journeys. Where they have been and what has happened that has shaped the direction of their lives? Participants are invited to use art supplies to make their pictures colorful. We typically give people 20 minutes to create their picture. Next, each person has 5-7 minutes to describe the images on their River of Life in small groups or in the large group. Ask listeners to hold their questions or comments until everyone is done. If the group is too large for everyone to hear all of the stories, you can divide up into groups of 5 or 6. Debrief questions can include:

- What was it like for you to tell your story to this group?
- What was it like for you to hear all of these stories?
- What surprised you?
- What insights have you gained about our group?

24. **Two Minutes Uninterrupted Conversation.** (Open to Relationship, Open to Risk, Invite the 'Stranger,' Learn in Public) This activity enhances our ability to listen attentively even to someone with whom we strongly disagree, and even to cultivate curiosity in what they have to say. It is a simple way to demonstrate the power of listening, suspending judgment, acknowledging another's point of view and inquiry. It can be used as a stand-alone activity to demonstrate the power of learning in public, or as a preparatory exercise that comes before a group dialogue. Determine a fairly provocative question that will elicit opinionated conversation, such as: "Are things getting better or worse in our group/organization? Why?" People form pairs, sitting "knee to knee." Person A goes first, speaking for two minutes on her/his point of view to the question. Person B will simply listen. No speaking — none. After two minutes, call a close. Invite the speakers to thank their listeners. Switch. Person B speaks for two minutes on her/his point of view to the question. Person A simply listens. At the end of two minutes, call a close and invite speakers to thank their listeners.

Debrief the experience by first asking what it was like to speak uninterrupted for two minutes, then, what it was like to listen uninterrupted for two minutes. Some will love it, others won't. The debrief demonstrates that speaking and listening are two distinct tools we have at our disposal, and that contrary to common opinion, we can actually be quite good listeners even when we don't say a thing! Debrief questions should also include what people learned, both about communication and about the topic the question referred to. The activity can be followed by another round, where the listener poses ONE thoughtful question to the partner, either in service to her/his understanding, or in service to the speaker's learning. This part encourages curiosity and learning in public.

25. **Doing Conflict Better.** (Invite the 'Stranger,' Learn in Public, Open to Relationship, Open to Risk, Open to Collective Creativity, Act Together, Sustain the Work) If we are successful in inviting the 'stranger' or strange ideas, there is bound to be disagreement. Many of us run the other way when faced with conflict, but there are ways to do conflict better so that we all become smarter and can transform old patterns and past hurts into new possibilities. Some of the best conflict work is done by having a direct conversation, while remaining aware of our constructive and destructive behaviors in conflict. The Center for Conflict Dynamics (www.conflictdynamics. org) offers online a free, short Hot Buttons assessment that identi-

fies personal triggers so that people know where they might get "hooked" when engaging in a difficult conversation. The following ground rules or scripted statements can be used to begin a challenging conversation. The goals of doing conflict better are to improve the relationship by courageously running toward the roar together, to identify preferred and more effective ways of working together, and to learn something about ourselves, the other, and/or the topic. Done well, conflict conversations can produce some very creative outcomes.

- There is something important I'd like to discus. Is this a good time for you?
- I've observed... (something factual)
- And it makes me feel ___, because...
- I'm wondering what is going on for you when this happens...
- What I'd prefer is...

26. **Giving Effective Feedback.** (Build Trust, Open to Safety, Open to Relationship, Invite the 'Stranger,' Learn in Public, Act Together, Open to Risk, Open to Collective Creativity) The ability to give feedback effectively is vital to maintaining a Gracious Space of open and honest communication. Before giving feedback, consider your purpose and the specific actions you want to reinforce or correct. Choose words that will gain support and defuse defensiveness.

- Focus on behavior, not personality traits or attitudes
- Use "I" statements
- Refrain from words like always and never, as in "you always..."
- Specify behavior rather than generalizing about habits or personality traits
- Give the feedback as close as possible to the specific behavior
- Accept that a feedback process is two-way, and provide an opportunity for the receiver to state concerns or barriers to change
- Check back to be sure your message was heard and understood

27. **Receiving Feedback Effectively.** (Build Trust, Open to Safety, Open to Relationship, Invite the 'Stranger,' Learn in Public, Act Together, Open to Risk, Open to Collective Creativity) Hearing feedback about ourselves is not easy, but how else are we to learn about habits and patterns that we cannot see? It is often through others that

we learn the deepest lessons about ourselves. Much of the time we add our own interpretations and judgment to feedback, but the more we can focus on behavior, the more we will be able to hear the intended message in a positive light.

- Assume the person providing feedback has your best interests at heart
- Assume the spirit of self-improvement and inviting the 'stranger'
- Be objective (if you were hearing this about someone else, would the way it's being given feel appropriate?)
- Take time to digest the information and ask for clarification and examples
- Check to be sure you understand the feedback and the goals for improvement
- Thank the person for caring enough to talk with you directly

28. **Asking Compelling Questions.** (Invite the 'Stranger,' Co-Construct Shared Purpose and Plans, Act Together, Sustain the Work, Learn in Public) This is a challenging activity that helps to bridge differences and open up possibilities through the process of formulating a purposeful question. The process of crafting a Compelling Question identifies the inherent (and sometimes opposing) values within an issue, and then forms a question that incorporates, bridges and builds on those values, with enough possibility to create direction and enough specificity to create traction.

Form small groups of 4-7, organized around a particular issue. All groups can take on the same issue, or groups can take on different issues under a theme. Each group is tasked with forming a compelling question. All participants first write down the two or three values they care about with respect to the issue. For example, if the issue is about a town's energy future, values could include an environmentally clean system, not too expensive, within their own control. Next, people take turns sharing with their small group the values they wrote down. (This could be done using versions of Two Minutes of Uninterrupted Listening, and Yes And.) As they are listening, invite members to keep track of common values. After each person has shared her/his values, ask the group to identify the 2-4 most important values to focus on. The group will then begin to craft a compelling question. It can be helpful to share some examples (which can be found at the beginning of this chapter).

Give groups 30-60 minutes to construct a question. Once questions are formed, ask the groups to post and share their questions in the large group. From here, the whole group or facilitator can choose one question (or a combination) that most adequately expresses the issue they need to discuss. Finally, the dialogue about the question begins. Most groups find that by the time they come to the dialogue, they have already found new perspective and common ground through the question-forming process. For this reason, the compelling question activity is a superb set-up for helping people to have dialogue about a difficult topic.

29. **Self-Preparation.** (Spirit — morning meditation) Sit quietly and relax the body, emotions and mind by breathing out any tensions and breathing in the quality of calm. Now think of people with whom you currently have difficulty in your relationships. See them as doing the best they can given their circumstances and, in a spirit of compassion and forgiveness, send thoughts of loving acceptance to them. Visualize the relationships as healing and renewing. Now take time to look inside yourself and note those aspects that you have not yet fully appreciated and accepted and send love and forgiveness to this inner family. Visualize the day ahead with all its potential interactions as a real opportunity for mindful practice. Know and affirm that through practice, Gracious Space grows each day as a positive force for good in the world.

30. **Self-Preparation.** (Spirit — evening review) Sit quietly and breathe out any tensions that may have accumulated in the body, emotions and mind during the day and breathe in a quality of calm. Reflect on the day by reviewing each interaction (moving back in time from now to the start of the day) and simply note, without blame or judgment, the quality of those interactions. Reflect on the degree to which you were able to live in Gracious Space with yourself and others. Note the impressions and give thanks for this day of learning. Finally, choose what will be different tomorrow as a result of what was learned today and then go to sleep holding that intent clearly in your heart and mind.

Summary

There are many ways to create Gracious Space, and we invite practitioners of Gracious Space to start with what they know and use these activities to guide a group forward. The purpose of this chapter is to describe some specific activities to establish Gracious Space. Most of these activities are described more fully on the Center's website, and several of them are accompanied by full facilitator guides. To find these and more tools and activities, please visit the Gracious Space Practitioner's Page on the Center's website at www.ethicalleadership.org.

We also encourage practitioners to become active members of the national Gracious Space Practitioners Network. This network enables members to share activities and find ways to bring Gracious Space to their contexts. To join the network, visit the Community Learning Exchange at www.communitylearningexchange.org. Click on "groups" and click again on the Gracious Space group. Proceed with instructions to join.

Conclusion

"The space within us and the space among us are the same space."

— *Henri Nouwen*

Gracious Space has the power to transform us individually and collectively. It does this by offering individuals and groups a way to navigate the space Henri Nouwen is talking about in this opening quote. His quote reminds us of the I/We connection — that the "I" impacts the "we," and the "we" impacts the "I." We know from long experience that when we disregard this reality we come up short on possibilities, and we can also do harm to others and ourselves. How we treat each other in the "in between" space affects our own inner journeys and the opposite is necessarily also true.

When the space between us is dominated by acts that diminish us, people will not bring their full passion, gifts, and energy to their work. Autocratic supervisors can get work accomplished in the short run; autocratic parents can gain compliance of their children in the short run. But this approach does not create capacity for long-term growth. If we have been diminished or wounded by another, we carry this wound inside, and it shapes our inner space and conversation. If the wounds are not healed, or if the energy is not transformed into something more positive, the wounds will show up in every group we become part of, affecting the way we interact with others and what is possible through us. The wounds that reside within us also reside in the spaces between us.

We can't afford to have people withdraw or become invisible. Our world needs the full talent and wisdom of all members of our communities and organizations. When we treat others with respect and understanding, we support a positive inner dialogue that shows up in positive relationships with others. We need to attend to the inner- and in-between spaces to bring out these gifts, and this is what Courageous Collaboration with Gracious Space is all about.

Peter Senge, a respected thought leader in the field of leadership and change, recently observed that the top leadership skill needed for our times is continuous learning. This skill enables us to see old habits and patterns that are harmful, and to shift into more healthy and sustainable patterns. During a visit to Seattle, Senge said, "We need to develop practices to unveil the system through relating and conversation. The types of conversations we have and the people we converse with color our points of view. The only way to escape our history is through collaborative reflection."

Using the Gracious Space Change Framework to its greatest potential means having these learning conversations and reflecting collaboratively. It means showing up with all of ourselves, being "all in" and committing fully and courageously to positive outcomes. To practice Courageous Collaboration with Gracious Space is to commit ourselves completely — to ourselves, to others and to the worthy possibilities for change that matter most.

The Gracious Space Change Framework enables us to develop individual and group capacity to run toward the roar, to inquire into the unknown, and to advance creative and positive change for the common good. The Framework is intended to hold our most complex change processes and the full range of dynamics that show up in communities and organizations. Using Gracious Space as a framework for change opens people up in a way that makes transformation more likely.

The Framework invites groups and individuals to restore wholeness to people, communities and organizations that have been wounded by hurtful patterns and institutions. The Framework helps leaders attend to a world that has been fragmented by unchecked self-interest and predominance of "I"-"It" consciousness and separation. The Framework can bring new connections, new life and restructuring to systems that have been damaged, and can bring healing and renewal to the individuals within the system. We have witnessed these breakthroughs again and again. We have also witnessed the fact that if we can see it, we can do it. As you begin or deepen your journey into Gracious Space, we offer again what has become a mantra for us and is reflected in the book title: Remember, it only takes a small opening for profound change to occur.

The Gracious Space Story

At a recent seminar conducted by Jet City Improv, Andrew McMaster taught us a very effective and entertaining way to tell a story. Stories should have seven parts, he said, and start with these lines: Once upon a time; and every day; until one day; because of this; and because of this; until finally; and ever since then. So we will use this template to tell the Gracious Space story, and at the end, invite readers to add a chapter of their own.

1. Once upon a time, in the early 1990s, Dr. William J. Grace (Bill) founded the Center for Ethical Leadership in Seattle. Bill was passionate about bringing leaders together to promote the common good and began to develop a series of programs around that mission.

2. And every day, he and the staff at the Center developed and hosted events to bring leaders together, teach them some skills, and convene projects on behalf of the common good.

3. Until one day, Bill's friend Jim Emrich used the term "gracious space" at a conference where he wanted to create a sense of hospitality for college students. Jim defined gracious space as "a place where the stranger feels welcome," and attributed the language to his friend Charlie Olsen. Bill found the term helpful to describe the kind of setting we were trying to create, where people could explore aspects of the common good. He and Pat Hughes, then serving as Director of Curriculum Development, began assembling a framework to describe a leader's pathway in service of the common good, using Gracious Space as a cornerstone.

Bill and Pat created a nine-month program called the Citizen Leaders Institute (CLI) around leadership for the common good. The program brought together leaders from business, government, education, human service, and religious sectors, to promote the common good together. Gracious Space was an effective way to create welcoming norms for 'strangers' to be together. Gracious Space brought those voices into the discussion, and provided an environment for examining the policies, systems and realities that threatened the good for some of our citizens and employees. CLI was successful, and the Center went on to develop workshops about leadership for the common good, including one on Creating Gracious Space.

4. Because of this, The Center developed the curriculum around Gracious Space more fully, and began to use Gracious Space with more programs. This included the Confluence, an innovative program to increase community capacity to tackle complex social issues by offering a format for bridging boundaries and collaborating in new ways. The Center also embarked on writing the first book on Gracious Space, which was published in 2004. It has sold over 8,000 copies and is in its third printing and second edition.

5. And because of this, Gracious Space became even more visible nationally. The Center brought Gracious Space to its role as the lead consulting organization for the Kellogg Foundation's Kellogg Leadership for Community Change program. In KLCC, Dale Nienow and Karma Ruder brought Gracious Space to vigorous life in eleven communities over the course of seven years. Gracious Space is now a core part of the national Community Learning Exchange, an extension of the Kellogg work that continues to foster dialogues and collaborative action around important social issues. Pat Hughes and others continued to use Gracious Space with organizations which were engaged in cultural change.

6. Until finally, the Center was ready to share what it had learned about applying Gracious Space to collaborative and transformational change processes. A second book project was conceived and begun in 2007 to reflect this learning. The development of this original thinking resulted in this book on the Gracious Space Change Framework, <u>Courageous Collaboration with Gracious Space: From Small Openings to Profound Transformation.</u>

7. And ever since then, the Gracious Space Change Framework is being used by hundreds of practitioners to catalyze and lead change in Gracious Space. We have a network of practitioners that spans the United States and several countries, and the Center consults with a variety of organizations to help bring Gracious Space to their work. The rest of the story is unfolding now. You are part of it! As you experiment with and use Gracious Space in your change contexts, we invite you to write to us about your results and learnings. Stay tuned for more exciting plot developments and twists of fate as we continue to co-create Gracious Space.

The End. For now.

Bibliography

Block, Peter. Community: The Structure of Belonging. San Francisco: Berrett-Koehler Publishers, 2008.

Bohm, David, and Mark Edwards. Changing Consciousness: Exploring the Hidden Source of Social, Political and Environmental Crises Facing Our World. San Francisco: Harper, 1991.

Brown, Michael. The Presence Process: A Healing Journey into Present Moment Awareness. Vancouver, BC: Namaste Publishing & New York: Beaufort Books, 1995.

Buber, Martin. I and Thou. Trans. Walter Kauffman. New York: Charles Scribner's Sons, 1970.

Collins, Jim, and Jerry I. Porras. Built to Last: Successful Habits of Visionary Companies. New York: HarperCollins, 1994.

Craik, Dinah. A Life for a Life. 1859.

Fowler, James, & Nicholas Christakis. "Cooperative Behavior Cascades in Human Social Networks." Proceedings of the National Academy of Sciences. 23 Mar 2010. 5334–5338

Goleman, Daniel. Emotional Intelligence: Why it Can Matter More than IQ. New York: Bantam Books, 1995.

---. Social Intelligence: The New Science of Human Relationships. New York: Bantam Books, 2006.

Hammer, Michael and James Champy. Reengineering the Corporation: A Manifesto for Business Revolution. New York: HarperCollins, 2001.

His Holiness the 14th Dalai Lama. "Public Address." Seeds of Compassion Conference, Seattle. April 2008.

Hughes, Patricia with Bill Grace. Gracious Space: A Practical Guide for Working Better Together. Seattle: Center for Ethical Leadership, 2004.

Hüther, Gerald. The Compassionate Brain: How Empathy Creates Intelligence. Trans. Michael H. Kohn. Boston: Trumpeter Books, 2006.

Jones, DeWitt. Everyday Creativity (DVD). Dewitt Jones Productions, 1999.

Macy, Joanna and Molly Young Brown. Coming Back to Life: Practices to Reconnect Our Lives, Our World. Gabriola Island, BC: New Society Publishers, 1998.

Maltz, Dr. Maxwell. Psycho Cybernetics. New York: Pocket Books, 1960.

Maslow, Abraham H. "A Theory of Human Motivation." Psychological Review. 50. 1943. 370-396.

McDaniel Jr., Reuben R., Michelle E. Jordan and Brigitte F. Fleeman. "Surprise, Surprise, Surprise! A Complexity Science View of the Unexpected." Health Care Management Review. Dec 2003 28(3): 266-278.

Mead, Margaret. Sex and Temperament in Three Different Societies. New York: HarperCollins, 1963.

Meade, Michael. The World Behind the World. Seattle: Greenfire Press, 2008.

Moss Kanter, Dr. Rosabeth. "Keynote Address." Blazing the Trail Community Leadership Association Conference, Fort Worth, Texas. Apr 2010.

Roddick, Anita. Business As Unusual: The Journey of Anita Roddick and the Body Shop. Chichester, UK: Anita Roddick Publishing, 2005.

Satir, Virginia. Conjoint Family Therapy. Palo Alto: Science and Behavior Books, 1983.

Scharmer, Dr. C. Otto. Theory U: Leading from the Future as It Emerges. San Francisco: Berrett-Koehler Publishers, 2007.

Schön, Donald. The Reflective Practitioner: How Professionals Think in Action. New York: Basic Books, 1983.

Schnarch, David. <u>Passionate Marriage: Keeping Love and Intimacy Alive in Committed Relationships.</u> New York: W.W. Norton & Company, 2009.

Senge, Peter. "Economic Success in Times of Change." Northwest Leadership Summit, Seattle Town Hall. May 2009.

Senge, Peter, C. Otto Scharmer, Joseph Jaworski and Betty Sue Flowers. <u>Presence: An Exploration of Profound Change in People, Organizations and Society.</u> Cambridge: Society for Organizational Learning, 2004.

Stein, Steven and Howard E. Book. <u>The EQ Edge: Emotional Intelligence and Your Success.</u> Hoboken: Jossey-Bass Publishers, 2000.

Tavris, Carol and Elliot Aronson. <u>Mistakes Were Made (but not by me): Why We Justify Foolish Beliefs, Bad Decisions and Hurtful Acts.</u> Orlando: Houghton Mifflin Harcourt, 2007.

Tuckman, Bruce. "Developmental Sequence in Small Groups." <u>Psychological Bulletin</u>. 63. 1965. 384-99.

Tutu, Desmond. <u>No Future Without Forgiveness</u>. New York: Doubleday, 1999.

Wallas, Graham. <u>Art of Thought.</u> New York: Harcourt, Brace & Company, 1926.

Wooldridge, Adrian. "Remembering Drucker." <u>The Economist</u>. 19 Nov 2009. 70.

About the Center for Ethical Leadership

The Center for Ethical Leadership cultivates leadership and builds the capacity for change, by helping organizations and communities tap local wisdom in service of the common good. We invite people to reach across boundaries, build trust, and lead from their core values to advance change. By convening diverse perspectives — especially those historically excluded — we are creating healthier, more just and inclusive communities.

We are the pioneering ethical leadership organization in the Pacific Northwest, building collective leadership capacity for those advancing social change around the country. Founded in 1991 by Dr. Bill Grace, the Center has engaged thousands of people across the United States and from more than 35 countries.

The Center frequently brings diverse people together to learn, explore and work for the common good. We create the conditions for personal and collective transformation through innovative models, programs and approaches such as Gracious Space. Our approach to leadership has proven effective in a variety of settings, including tribal nations, rural communities, urban neighborhoods, communities of color and nonprofit organizations.

Our collective leadership and community change work across the country led to the founding of the Community Learning Exchange in 2008. This network brings together resilient communities, vibrant organizations and active change agents to share their local wisdom and collective leadership approaches with each other so they can be more effective in addressing critical social issues. You can join this network of change agents at www.communitylearningexchange.org.

The Center is a nonprofit corporation in the State of Washington. Visit us at www.ethicalleadership.org, call 206-328-3020, or visit us on Facebook.

Pat Hughes is the primary author of <u>Gracious Space: A Practi-cal Guide for Working Better Together</u>, published in 2004 by the Center for Ethical Leadership. Pat serves as senior partner for the Center's national Gracious Space Initiative, teaching and facilitating on Gracious Space across the country and providing support to hundreds of prac-titioners. She specializes in helping groups have honest conversations and reach their full potential. The Community Leadership Association named Pat one of it's first Preceptor Award winners in 1995, and the City of Redmond named her a Distinguished Leader in 1998. Pat has a Master's degree in Whole Systems Design/Organization Development from Seattle's Antioch University, and a Bachelor's degree in Economics and International Relations from the University of New Hampshire.

Karma Ruder is the Director for Community Collaboration at the Center for Ethical Leadership. Karma has worked in public and non-profit sectors, designing processes which inspire people to move beyond differences and conflict into the creative territory of commu-nity and collaboration. As co-leader of the national Kellogg Leadership for Community Change project to develop collective, place-based lead-ership, Karma served as lead author for the <u>Framework Workbook</u> and lead editor for <u>The Collective Leadership Storybook: Weaving Strong Communities</u>. Karma works with local and regional change initiatives, where she specializes in deepening and spreading Gracious Space and collective leadership. Previously, she directed the City of Seattle's Neighborhood Planning Office, which engaged 30,000 citizens in creat-ing plans for growing with grace, guiding over $500 million in City investments. She has a Master's Degree in Public Administration and a Bachelor's in Philosophy and Human Relations, both from the Univer-sity of Kansas.

Dr. Dale Nienow is the Executive Director of the Center for Ethi-cal Leadership. A consultant, leader and educator, Dale is known for helping people open up to deeper dialogue and new relationships that will move groups and communities forward on their compelling issues. He helps people work together across boundaries to include diverse perspectives, particularly those historically excluded. Dale co-led the Kellogg Leadership for Community Change program on behalf of the W. K. Kellogg Foundation and is one of the founders of the national Community Learning Exchange. He serves on a variety of community boards and consults frequently with a broad range of organizations across sectors. Dale has a Ph.D. in Education from the University of Southern California, a Master's degree in Administration from Pacific Lutheran University, and Bachelor's degree in Economics from St. Olaf College.

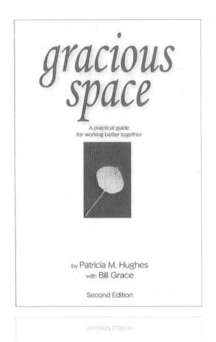

Gracious Space: A practical guide for working better together, by **Pat Hughes with Bill Grace.** This book describes the four elements of Gracious Space – spirit, setting, invite the 'stranger,' and learn in public. Learn how these elements create a holding environment that supports working and learning together.

The Collective Leadership Storybook: Weaving Strong Communities, edited by **Karma Ruder.** This book describes the patterns of working together that encourage collective leadership. Read about communities where people have made these patterns a way of life to advance the common good.

To order these, or any of our publications, please visit our website.
www.ethicalleadership.org